The Technique
of Branscombe
Point Lace

PHOTOGRAPH 1 *Mrs Olive Warren's cottage, where she taught her niece and the author to make Branscombe Point lace*

The Technique of Branscombe Point Lace

Lillie D. Trivett

B.T. BATSFORD LIMITED · LONDON

Dedicated in remembrance of two Branscombe ladies: Auntie Somers (Mrs Laura Somers) and Auntie Olive (Mrs Olive Warren). In the latter's cottage Freda (her niece) and myself spent many happy evenings learning the techniques of Branscombe Point lace.

© Lillie D. Trivett 1991

First published 1991

ISBN 0 7134 6761 4

Typeset by Lasertext Ltd., Longford Trading Estate,
Thomas Street, Stretford, Manchester M32 0JT.

and printed in Great Britain by
Courier International, Tiptree, Essex
for the Publisher
B. T. Batsford Ltd
4 Fitzhardinge Street
London W1H 0AH

Contents

Acknowledgements

My sincere thanks to the *Express & Echo*, Exeter, for allowing me to use their copyright to reproduce PHOTOGRAPH 2. Also to Pat Earnshaw for allowing me to use her copyright to reproduce PHOTOGRAPH 15. Also to Ronald Brown for his excellent photographs and Graham Searle for his superb line drawings.

For allowing me to photograph lace my thanks to: Mrs Chris Corbyn, PHOTOGRAPHS 17 and 18; Miss Anne Durham, PHOTOGRAPH 98; Miss Helen Gracey, PHOTOGRAPH 35; Mrs Jane Hooper, PHOTOGRAPH 37; Mrs L. Lindsell, PHOTOGRAPH 97; Mr Jeremy Pearson (Exeter Museum), PHOTOGRAPH 25; Mrs Joan Ridge, PHOTOGRAPHS 40, 103 and 104; Mrs Joy Tedbury, PHOTOGRAPHS 26 and 27; Miss Maureen Veal, PHOTOGRAPH 95; Mrs M. Wakley, PHOTOGRAPH 33 and Mrs Carol Williamson, PHOTOGRAPHS 9 and 10.

Grateful thanks to Mrs Caroline Ellis, Mrs E. Ellis, Mrs L. Lindsell and Mrs M. Morton for their help.

I am indebted to Mrs H. Barton for all her help and encouragement and to Mrs Margaret Tomlinson for PHOTOGRAPHS 3–8, 19–21, 23 and 30–31, and for information about her family.

To Mrs Bidney Maunsell, PHOTOGRAPHS 11–14, 24, 32 and 39, a friend with a wealth of knowledge about lace, always willing to give help and invaluable advice.

For typing: Mrs Vera Hills and Miss Jo Truby.

For reading the typescript: Miss Mo Gibbs, Chairman of the Lace Guild; Miss Lyn Godfrey and Mrs Peggy Sturgiss.

Quotations on p. 15: Devon Record Office.

The illustrations seen on the part-title pages are repeats of patterns to be found elsewhere in the book, where full captions and/or instructions are given.

Foreword

I was born in Colyton in Devon, a small town renowned for its lacemakers and traders, and was introduced to lacemaking at the age of five. Living next door to a lacemaker and having been given a pillow (pilla) and bobbins (lace-sticks) I soon learnt how to make braid. I married into a well-known lacemaking family and during the 1950s and 1960s lived in the coastal village of Branscombe where I had the pleasure of knowing several lacemakers intimately.

I often chatted to Mrs Lucy Hutchings who owned the village cornershop and was very good at designing lace patterns. Her sister, Mrs Rose Perryman, repaired lace, a skill she had learnt from my mother-in-law's sister, Hilda Dowell. I now regret not having watched more closely to learn how lace was repaired.

My father-in-law worked for Mr and Mrs Clement Ford at 'The Look Out' (the coastguard cottages) and my husband was often called upon by Mr Ford — sometimes during the night — to free rubbish from the turbine which supplied his electricity. This turbine was fed by the village stream.

The Ford, Tucker and Chick families of Branscombe had a long association with dealing in the lace trade. A descendant, Mrs Margaret Tomlinson, published a very interesting book in 1983 entitled, *Three Generations in the Honiton Lace Trade*.

After the Second World War, the braid needed for making Branscombe Point was almost unobtainable and during the early 1960s, the Branscombe branch of the Women's Institute (W.I.) put out an appeal. The very good response provided them with several different types of braid.

In the late 1960s I realized that Branscombe Point lacemaking was a dying craft. It was at this time that I was given by Mrs Dean (wife of the head gardener for the Chick family) an old biscuit tin containing – amongst other things – Branscombe Point patterns, braids, cords and cottons. Furthermore, in the book *Lace Making and Collecting* by A. Penderel Moody, I read: 'Perhaps a return to the old Tape Lace would set the Branscombe workers on their feet again, for their Point Lace stitches are too good to be lost'. Thus my interest was aroused. In my Honiton Lace class I mentioned it to a friend, Freda, and we decided to learn all we could about Branscombe Point lace and its stitches from Freda's Aunt, Mrs Olive Warren.

Auntie Olive and Laura Somers (Auntie Somers), even then both well into their 70s, taught us all the stitches they could remember. Auntie Olive had learnt the stitches as a child from a local farmer's wife. Mrs Somers, at an early age, was given one penny (old money) for tacking braid on to a pattern and overcasting. After learning filling stitches from a cousin, she was paid six pennies for a small doily. She also made black lace for evening garments. Sadly, very little black lace has survived, owing to a defect in the dyeing process which caused the lace to rot.

PHOTOGRAPH 2 *Mrs Laura Somers with a neighbour, Miss Elsie Parrett, making Branscombe Point on 30 August 1966. (Reproduced by kind permission of the* Express & Echo)

Part 1

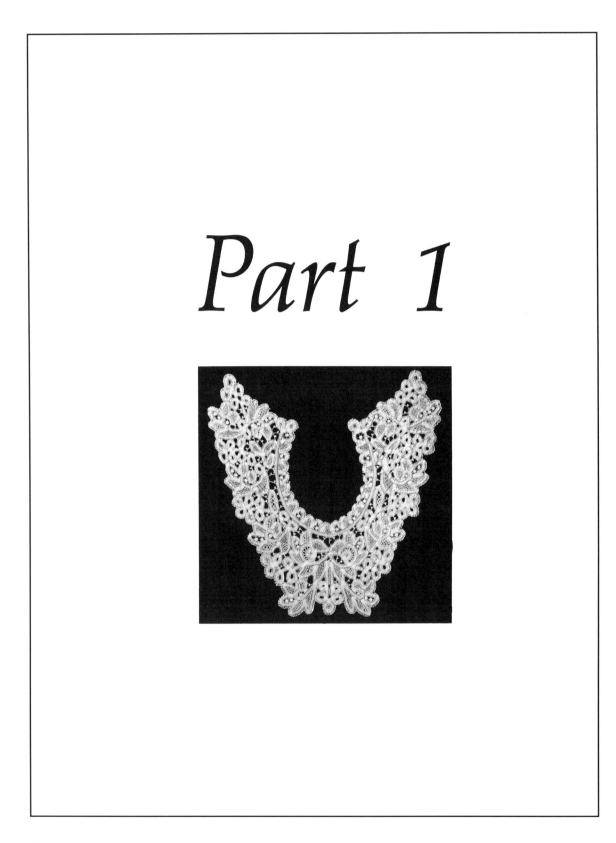

Branscombe village

Branscombe is reputed to be the longest village in East Devon and still contains many old and interesting buildings, including St Winifred's Church, in and around which can be found the names of many lacemakers and the thatched smithy, where many a visitor has bought a horseshoe made by the blacksmith, Harry Lazel. Mr Lazel was also a chimney-sweep and the village postman and his wife was a lacemaker. The bakery opposite the smithy was owned by the Collier family for generations where they baked bread in the old ashen faggot oven. Once a year, using apples given by the farmers, they baked huge apple pies which were carried on horse-drawn wagons to the village square on Apple Pie Fayre Day. The property is now owned by The National Trust who have opened the bakery as tea-rooms for the public.

Branscombe was also famous for early potatoes, broadbeans and strawberries, which were grown in little plots on ledges of the frost-free south-facing cliffs. During the winter months, donkeys carrying panniers hauled seaweed up the steep cliff paths, where it was dug into the soil.

The Sea Shanty Café, at Branscombe Mouth, was once a walled-in coal dump where stout-bottomed boats brought coal from South Wales. Just above the Sea Shanty, on the cliff, stands 'The Look Out', a row of coastguard cottages, which were the residence of Mr Ford (who died in 1961) and are now a hotel. Mr Ford had owned most of Branscombe, but after his death, the farmers were given the opportunity to purchase their farms, and much of Branscombe became part of the National Trust.

PHOTOGRAPHS 3 and 4 *Early Branscombe Point lace from the Tucker workrooms, showing good quality narrow braids*

Lace traders

The Tucker family, of 'Barnells' were selling needlelace known as 'Branscombe' by 1860, and importing the tape from Paris. They are known to have travelled to and from the Continent and are thought to have been responsible for introducing Branscombe Point to the UK, after acquiring ideas from Italian and French tape laces.

PHOTOGRAPH 5 *Lace from the Tucker workrooms*

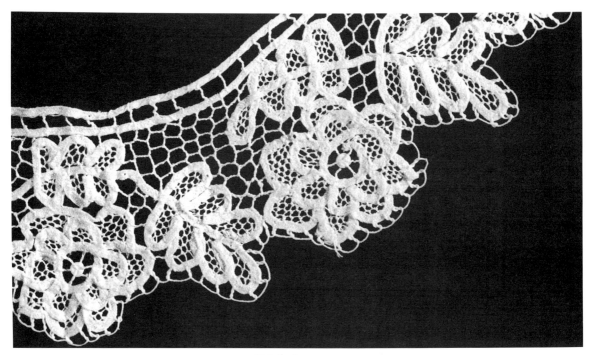

PHOTOGRAPH 6 *Detail of* PHOTOGRAPH 5

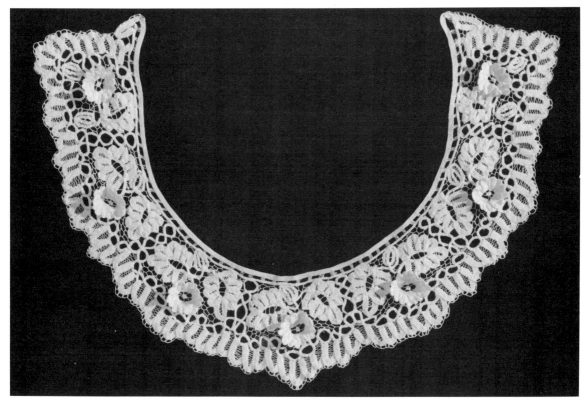

PHOTOGRAPH 7 *Early Branscombe Point of fine quality*

Ford family letters refer to the quality of the braid, or tape. For example:

7th June 1860

Dear Mary,
The 50 dozen No. 3 comes straight from Paris direct and must be kept, good or bad. Perhaps you had better see part of it before I send No. 4.

and

Dear Mary,
I send you another lot of braid, which happily came last evening. I hope it is better than the last.

PHOTOGRAPHS 3–10 show early Branscombe Point lace from the Tucker workrooms. The lace is made with very good quality braid, probably from France. Note there is no pinloop edge, and the braids are narrow. They may well be the same ones mentioned in the Ford

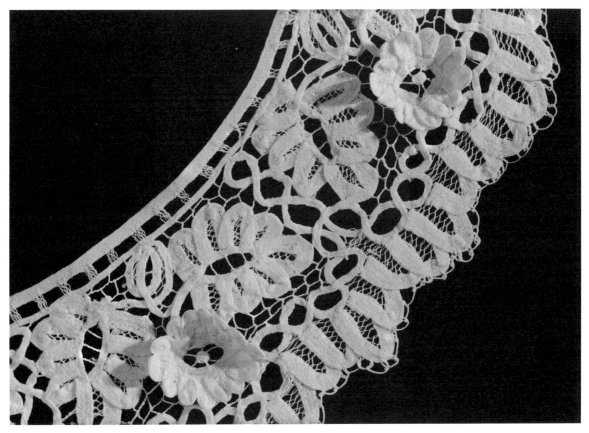

PHOTOGRAPH 8 *Detail of* PHOTOGRAPH 7 *showing raised flower petals*

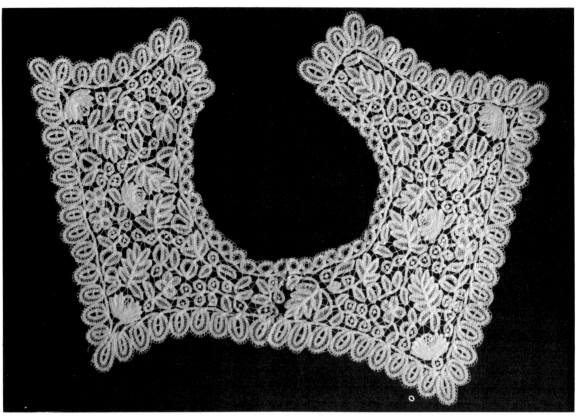

PHOTOGRAPH 9 *Closely designed early Branscombe Point using very narrow braid*

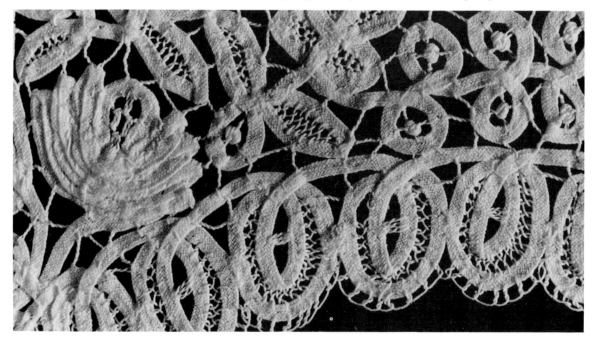

PHOTOGRAPH 10 *Flower detail of* PHOTOGRAPH 9

letter. Laces like those in the preceding photographs cannot be identified as Branscombe Point without knowing for sure that they were actually made in Branscombe, *and* knowing the identity of the lacemaker, as there were no fillings, only cutwork, connecting bars and loops.

PHOTOGRAPH 11

Mrs Ida Allen's Beer Lace Shop

PHOTOGRAPH 12 *Mrs Ida Allen, at the door of the Beer Lace Shop*

PHOTOGRAPH 13 *Branscombe Point bedspread from Mrs Allen's workroom*

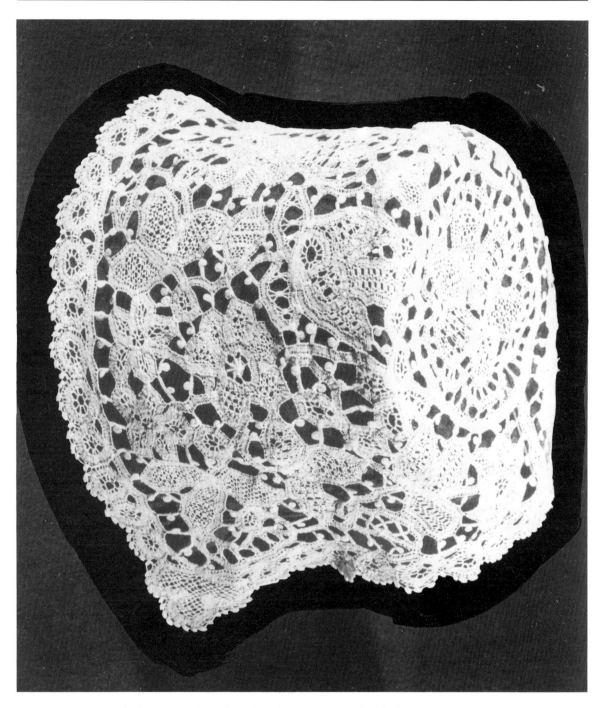

A well-known lady, Mrs Ida Allen, lived in Branscombe before acquiring the Lace Shop in the neighbouring village of Beer. PHOTOGRAPHS 11–14 show her shop and some of the lace that could be bought there. PHOTOGRAPHS 15 and 16 show the types of braid available at the time.

PHOTOGRAPH 14 *Baby's bonnet from Mrs Allen's shop*

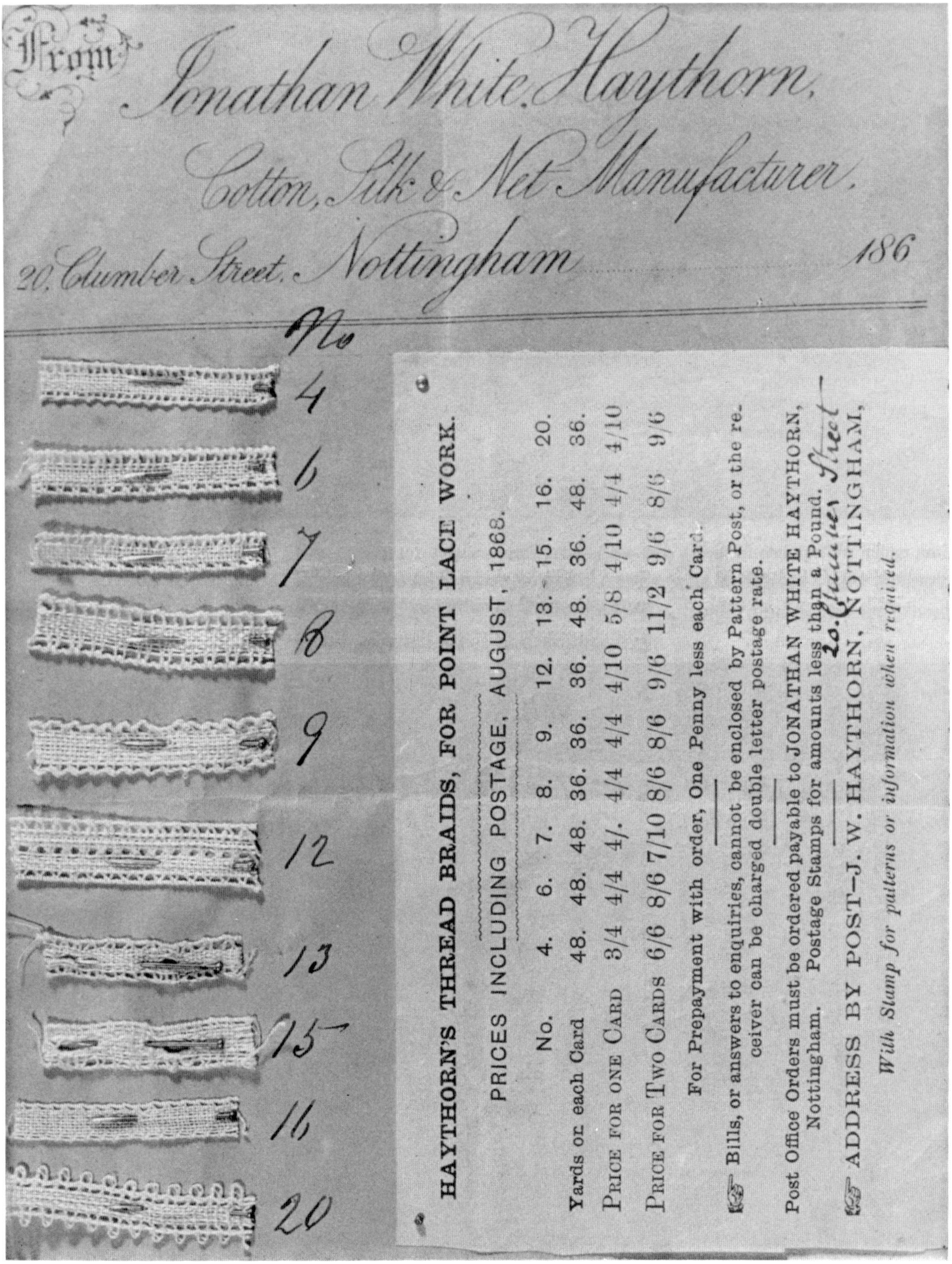

PHOTOGRAPH 15 *Haythorn of Nottingham dated 1868, supplier of braids. (Reproduced by kind permission of Pat Earnshaw)*

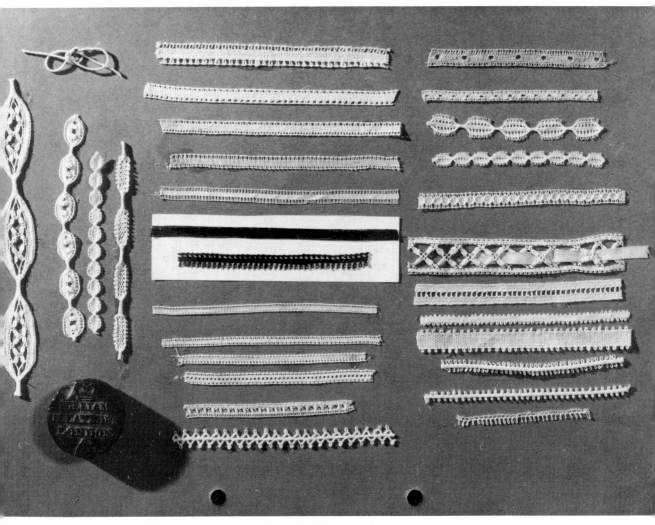

PHOTOGRAPH 16 *Assorted braids in author's possession, cobbler's wax and cord*

Traditional Branscombe Point

During the second half of the nineteenth century Branscombe Point lace gained recognition, and the industry did extremely well. Between 1870 and 1920 magazines and books became available which showed needlelace-making techniques and numerous exciting filling stitches. Some stitches were copies, some were invented variations.

Branscombe was made on brown paper with plain, straight-edged braids. Petal braids (PHOTOGRAPHS 32–34) were not used until plain

PHOTOGRAPH 17 *Cord was used for the outline of this design instead of braid*

PHOTOGRAPH 18 *Made by Emaline Newton for her confirmation in the late 1860s, this was placed on top of the head to crown a confirmation veil*

PHOTOGRAPH 19
For a confirmation veil

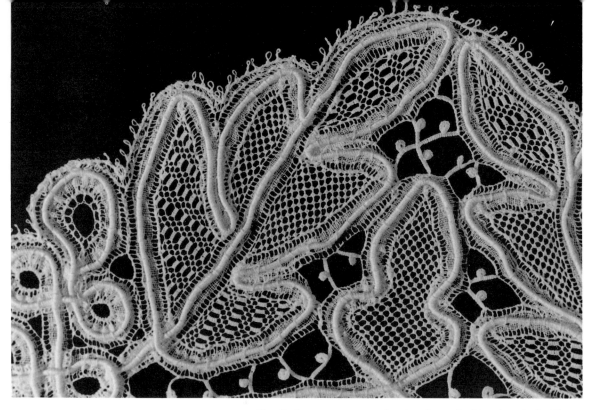

PHOTOGRAPH 20 *Detail of* PHOTOGRAPH 19, *showing the cord whipped to the braid*

PHOTOGRAPH 21 *Wrong side of* PHOTOGRAPH 19

braids became difficult to obtain during and after the Second World War. Patterns were guarded to prevent them being copied by one's neighbour.

The thread used was Tailor's cotton No. 10, but for fine work No. 11 or 12 was purchased, wound upon reels. Other threads used were Harris thread, purchased wound upon reels, in skeins or in balls and Haythorn's linen thread, which was sold in hanks of 600 yards (550 metres).

Some less popular Branscombe Point was made using a cord to outline the design instead of braid, PHOTOGRAPH 17 shows an example of this type made by Emaline Newton of Branscombe, during 1860. The butterfly antennae are made with milliner's wire.

PHOTOGRAPH 22 *A typical design of the late nineteenth century*

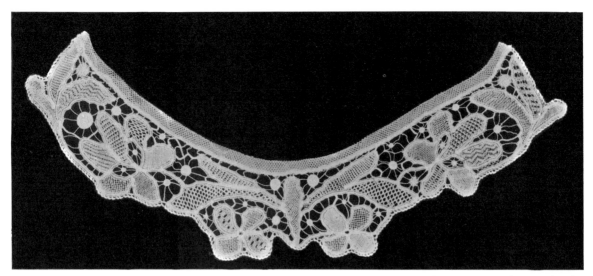

PHOTOGRAPH 23 *Late nineteenth-century, poor quality lace, connections between braids consisting of badly made Cutworks*

PHOTOGRAPH 24 *Early twentieth-century lace with various stitches, of superb, even workmanship*

PHOTOGRAPH 25 *Early twentieth-century lace with the popular tulip and rose design*

PHOTOGRAPH 26 *Black braid, with various filling stitches in pink and emerald-green silks*

PHOTOGRAPH 27 *Same design as* PHOTOGRAPH 26, *made in the early 1960s by Olive Warren after the W.I. appeal for braid*

PHOTOGRAPH 28 *Made by Laura Somers, 1973*

PHOTOGRAPH 29 *Made in 1973 this is a similar design to the handkerchief in* PHOTOGRAPH 31

PHOTOGRAPH 30 *Made between 1920 and 1935*

PHOTOGRAPH 31 *Corner detail of* PHOTOGRAPH 30

PHOTOGRAPH 32 *Branscombe Point made with petal braids made during or just after the Second World War*

PHOTOGRAPH 18 shows a piece of Branscombe Point (also made by Emaline Newton) that was worn on the head to crown a confirmation veil. Note how a cord has been whipped along the centre of the braid, giving the lace a more elaborate, raised effect. The triangular shape is symbolic of the triple personality of God. Only on ecclesiastical Branscombe Point have I come across the machine-made purl edge, instead of the familiar handmade purl edge.

PHOTOGRAPH 33 *Branscombe Point sampler using petal braids made during the 1960s by Laura Somers*

Honiton Point

Patterns for this needlepoint lace were printed on blue or green glazed linen. They were marked 'Honiton Point', and an indication was given of which number braid to use. Petal braid was incorporated into the patterns, as part of the design, sometimes for petals of a flower, or as leaves, as was the number for the machine purl edging to be attached.

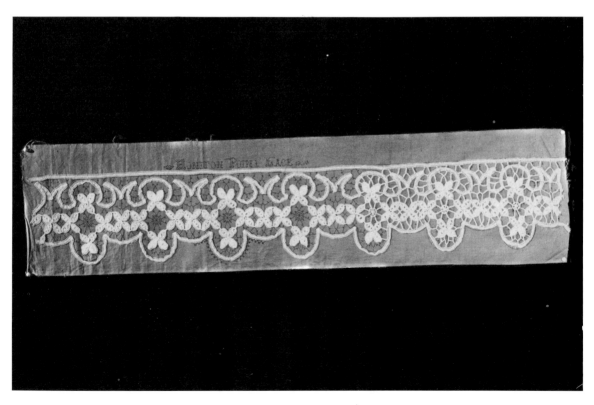

PHOTOGRAPH 34 *Honiton Point collar, petal braid being part of the design*

PHOTOGRAPHS 35 and 36 *Honiton Point in the making, on a blue glazed-linen pattern*

The following pattern (not Branscombe), like many others, can be adapted as shown:

PHOTOGRAPH 37 *Branscombe Point collar, adapted from a Honiton Point pattern*

DRAWING 1 *A tape-lace pattern being adapted for Branscombe Point*

DRAWING 2 *Old Peter Pan collar (design no. 158, by Penelope) adapted for Branscombe Point.*

Identifying Branscombe Point

To distinguish Branscombe Point lace and its patterns from other braid laces and patterns can be a problem for the inexperienced. In traditional Branscombe Point lace, the outer edge of the finished article usually has a very attractive handmade buttonhole stitch purl edging, each purl consisting of five buttonhole stitches. An insertion of Nibs filling – a purl (worked like the purl edge) – is made in the centre of a buttonhole stitch bar.

Although even today one comes across an enormous number of old braid or tape lace patterns, one rarely finds a traditional

PHOTOGRAPH 38 *Handkerchief showing the Purl edging and Nibs; the bars between the butterfly motif and the outer edge*

PHOTOGRAPH 39A *Handkerchief corner enlarged*

PHOTOGRAPH 39B *Wrong side of the corner*

Branscombe brown-paper pattern, or a dealer's pattern marked on thin leather. Very thin leather was used for the latter, especially for important orders, the pattern being drawn on to the leather with a red-hot needle or skewer. Colyton, five miles (eight kilometres) from Branscombe, still has one of the only two oak-bark tanneries left in Britain today, where one has always been able to purchase odd scraps of leather.

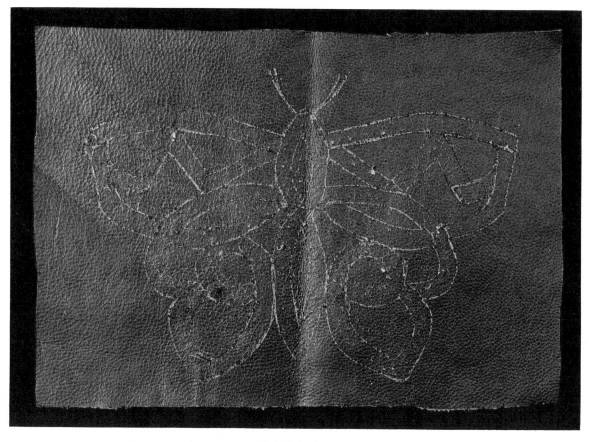

PHOTOGRAPH 40 *Dealer's leather pattern*

Part 2

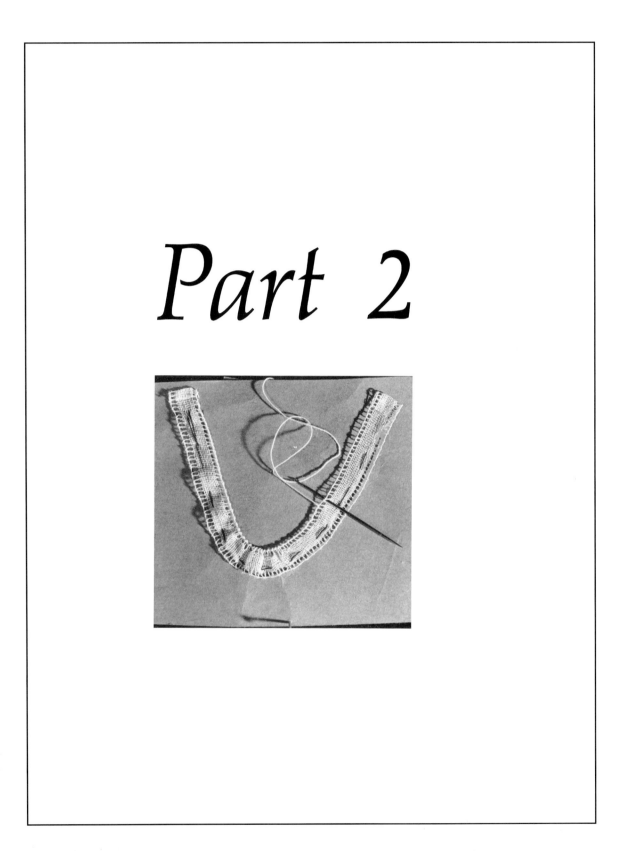

Equipment

The materials required are very few:

Braid:	Measure enough before starting to avoid joins
Thread:	Use cotton appropriate to the braid. Finer, strong cotton is advised for overcasting or whipping
Coloured thread:	Any odd colours of fine thread for tacking
Scissors:	Should be small, sharp and pointed
Thimble	
Drawing pencil	
Rubber	
Fine pen	
Needles:	No special kind is required, though some people prefer to use a ballpoint for the fillings. Personally I find ballpoint needles a nuisance. I was taught with an ordinary medium-size needle, turning it in reverse (i.e. using the eye first) for the overcasting and buttonhole stitches
Brown paper:	Must be good quality
Tracing paper:	An acceptable alternative is ordinary kitchen greaseproof paper
Plastic film:	Choose translucent, adhesive-backed in blue or green with a matt finish

Patterns

Traditionally, copies of patterns were made by taking heel-ball rubbings with cobbler's wax, after tacking the braid on to a pattern, and overcasting the inside edge of the braid. This was done before any filling stitches were worked in the spaces between the braids.

The prepared pattern was pinned on a flat surface and a thin piece of brown paper was placed on top and held down firmly. Heel-ball was then rubbed lightly over the brown paper, to obtain a copy of the pattern, i.e. the same method used for taking brass-rubbings.

PHOTOGRAPH 41 *Braid tacked and whipped onto pattern, ready to take a heel-ball rubbing*

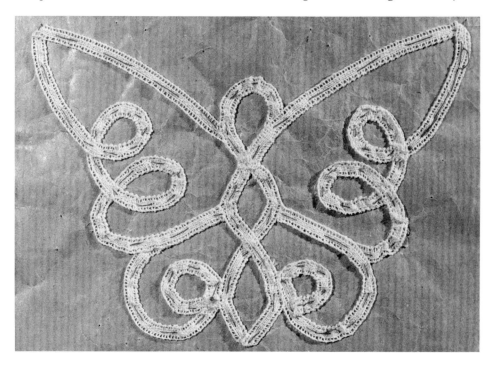

Preparation

With the availability of photocopying today there is no need to take rubbings for new patterns, especially since cobbler's wax can leave dirty marks on the lace.

A design on tracing paper can be photocopied on to brown paper, and the tracing kept for further patterns. Alternatively, the design can be traced on to a sheet of kitchen greaseproof paper. Then the ink side is placed down on two thicknesses of brown paper, with their shiny smooth sides uppermost.

After tacking the braid securely to the pattern, take a pair of scissors and snip the greaseproof in several places (taking care not to snip the braid) before pulling the greaseproof away, leaving the braid against the brown paper.

Another method uses blue, green or black translucent matt-finish plastic acetate film, which is adhesive on one side. Remove the protective backing and stick carefully on to the photocopied pattern or traced design, before placing on a piece of brown paper for backing, ready to tack on the braid.

Points to remember and working hints

1 Work must look lacey
2 Tension is very important
3 Avoid unnecessary joins in the braid by measuring enough braid for the pattern before starting
4 Keep the shiny or smooth surface of the brown paper uppermost
5 Use good quality (non fluffy) thread
6 Practise the stitches beforehand to find a grade of thread to suit the braid and stitch tension

Note: left-handed lacemakers will probably find it easier to work the given instructions in the opposite direction, i.e. right to left instead of left to right.

Beginning and finishing

Secure the thread with 2 or 3 tiny, tight, invisible buttonhole stitches into the braid.

Needle direction

Remember to always bring the needle from *beneath* the braid and *up* through the braid pinloops when overcasting.

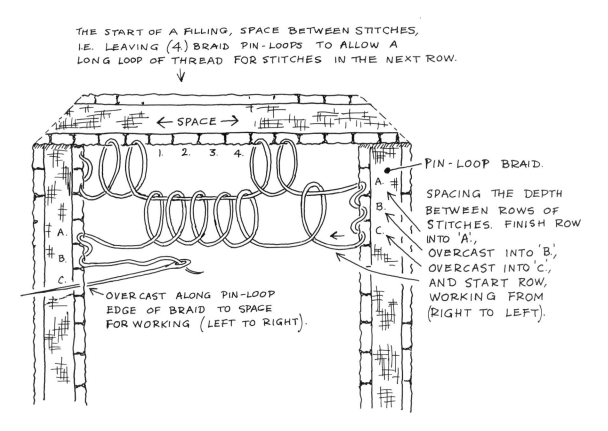

THE START OF A FILLING, SPACE BETWEEN STITCHES,
I.E. LEAVING (4.) BRAID PIN-LOOPS TO ALLOW A
LONG LOOP OF THREAD FOR STITCHES IN THE NEXT ROW.

← SPACE →

1. 2. 3. 4.

PIN-LOOP BRAID.

SPACING THE DEPTH
BETWEEN ROWS OF
STITCHES. FINISH ROW
INTO 'A.',
OVERCAST INTO 'B.',
OVERCAST INTO 'C.',
AND START ROW,
WORKING FROM
(RIGHT TO LEFT).

OVERCAST ALONG PIN-LOOP
EDGE OF BRAID TO SPACE
FOR WORKING (LEFT TO RIGHT).

DRAWING 3 *Spacing*

Spacing fillings

Overcast along the braid pinloops, taking into consideration the thickness of the threads being used and your tension. The distance between each row should be the same throughout the filling. The buttonhole stitches should all be the same size, and the loops between the stitches the same length.

Compare PHOTOGRAPHS 86, 87 and 88. 86 and 87 both show Linen stitch with cord, but PHOTOGRAPH 87, the variation stitch, is more openly spaced, as is PHOTOGRAPH 88 of Double Linen stitch with cord.

Thread

Start a new thread where two braids overlap, passing the needle between these 2 braids. On a single layer of braid, make tiny running or tacking stitches along the braid (to be cut and pulled out later) and along the braid pinloops, securing with a buttonhole stitch.

SECURE
WITH A TIGHT
BUTTON HOLE STITCH,
PERHAPS 2.

CUT END OF
NEW THREAD AFTER
FINISHING ROW OF STITCHES.

DRAWING 4 *New thread being secured on a single layer of braid*

Points and folded corners

For fillings starting from a point make a single thread bar-loop to take the first buttonhole stitch or stitches.

Removing lace from the pattern

When the lace is finished, cut the tacking stitches on the back of the brown paper. Take care when pulling out the tacks. Examine all the folds and connections in the braid, neatly overcasting or sewing together any that have been missed. Lay the lace upside down between two damp cloths, and press with a hot iron to make the overcast edge of curves and inside edges of the braid lie flat.

Remember that one works the lace on the wrong side. The right side of the work should be against the paper pattern.

Note: The shiny side of the brown paper is easier to work on, as the needle is apt to dig into the rough side, and minute pieces of paper sometimes get between the stitches.

Tacking the braid

Measure enough to avoid unnecessary joins and allow a little extra to fold over for a turning at the start and finish.

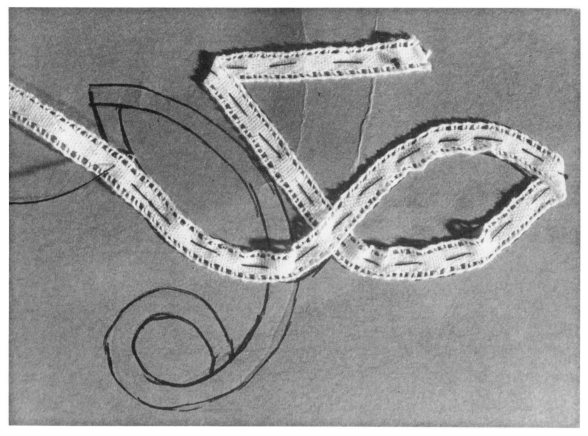

PHOTOGRAPH 42 *Tacking the braid on to a traced pattern*

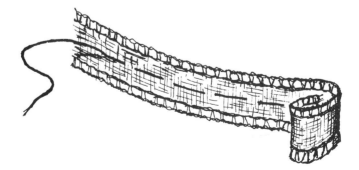

DRAWING 5 *Folding the braid*

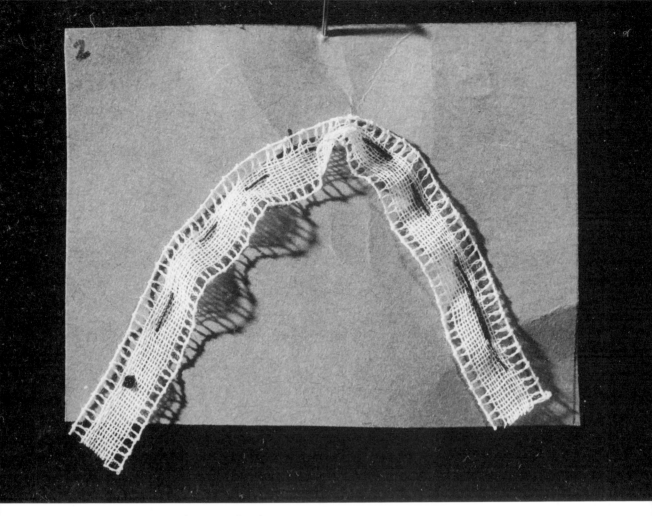

PHOTOGRAPH 43 *Tacking around curves and circles*

Loops and curves

Tack just off-centre, slightly closer to the outer edge of the curve, so that the braid gathers or puckers on the inner edge. The fullness will be drawn into shape when overcasting.

Points, sharp angles and corners

The braid must be neatly folded into shape and pressed firmly between the fingers before tacking securely. An extra stitch is often required to keep a firm shape.

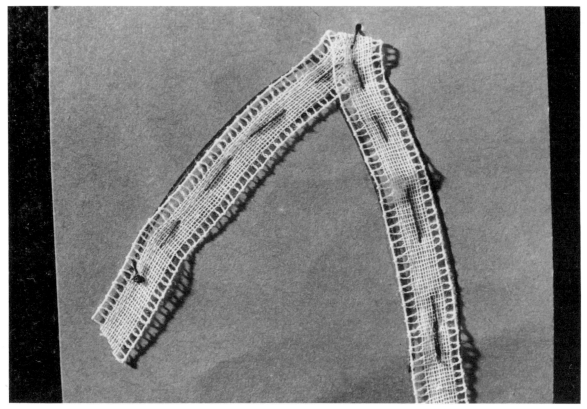

PHOTOGRAPH 44 *Folded corner with an extra tacking stitch on the point*

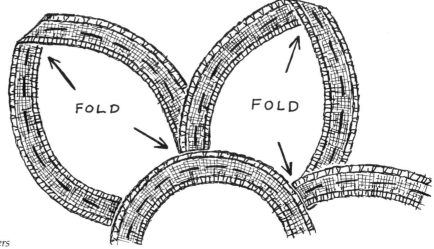

DRAWING 6 *Folding the braid on points, sharp angles and corners*

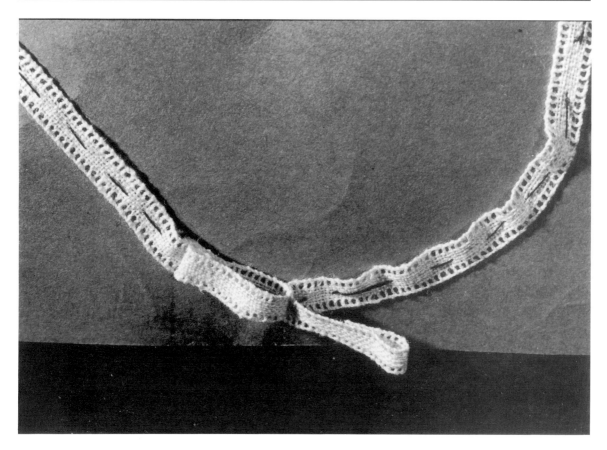

PHOTOGRAPH 45 *Joining the braid*

Joining the braid

Joins in the braid should be avoided, but when the necessity arises, the braids should be seamed together, opened, and the ends folded under and flattened carefully before sewing each portion down separately as neatly as possible.

DRAWING 7 *Joining or seaming braids together*

Finishing

Where two ends of the braid meet, such as in circles, fold the end of the bottom braid *up*, and the end of the top braid *down*. Lay one upon the other, and overcast neatly together.

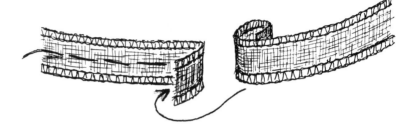

DRAWINGS 8 and 9 *show how two ends of braid are folded and connected at the finish, after tacking a design*

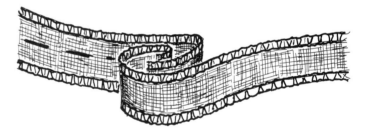

Overcasting or whipping

This is essential for every article, to achieve the foundation for the fillings and to reduce the fullness on the inner, curved edges.

Knots should not appear in the lace. Carefully attach the thread where braids overlap by drawing the thread between the braids just until the end disappears. Buttonhole stitch into the edge of the braid to secure it.

Alternatively, attach the thread by passing the needle downwards through a pinloop of the braid, leaving an end of cotton. Secure this by making tiny, tight buttonhole stitches into the edge of the braid. Cut off the end of the cotton. (*See* DRAWING 4, p. 45.)

Working left to right, overcast into each pinloop of the braid, pulling the thread gently every few stitches, like a gathering thread, so that the inner edge of the curves lies flat like the opposite outer edge.

Note: Do not overcast more than 1 stitch into any one braid pinloop, otherwise you will not be able to pull the thread.

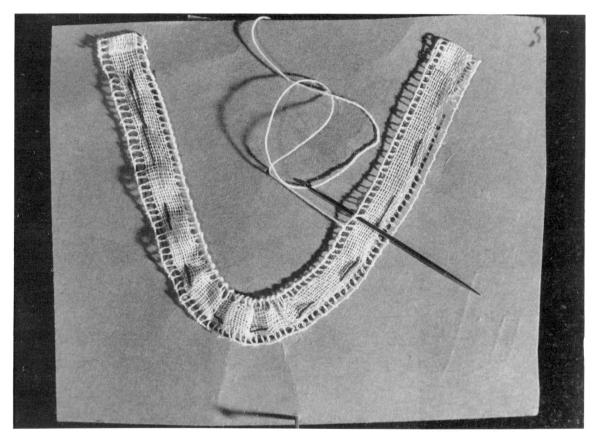

PHOTOGRAPH 46 *Overcasting on the inside edge of a curve, bringing the needle up through the braid pinloops, working left to right. This also shows the thread pulled after every few stitches*

Part 3

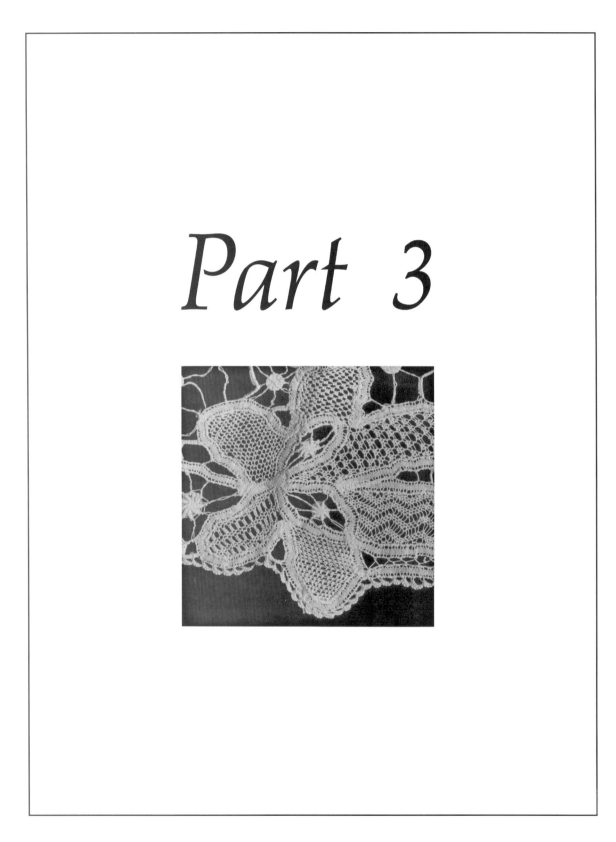

Filling stitches

Fillings, consisting mainly of buttonhole stitches, are worked to fill the spaces in the design. Remember to space fillings (*see* p. 44) and practise the various fillings beforehand, for a nice even tension.

Buttonhole stitch

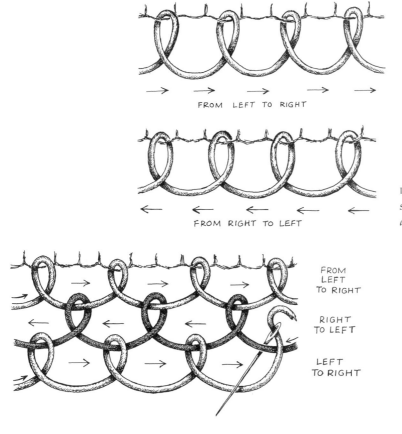

FROM LEFT TO RIGHT

FROM RIGHT TO LEFT

DRAWINGS 10 and 11 *Buttonhole stitches, from left to right and right to left*

FROM LEFT TO RIGHT

RIGHT TO LEFT

LEFT TO RIGHT

Double knot

Pairs of buttonhole stitches worked in rows, evenly spaced, from left to right, then right to left.

1st row: a single buttonhole stitch into each of 2 braid pinloops. Miss the next braid pinloop. Repeat to end of row, with a loop between each pair of stitches. *Secure* thread into braid. Overcast along to next braid pinloop, securing thread for the next row.

PHOTOGRAPH 47 *Double knot*

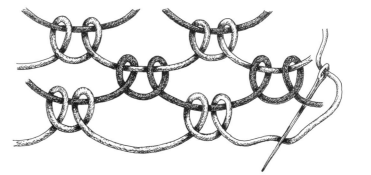

DRAWING 12 *Double knot*

2nd & repeat rows: into each loop (between the pairs of stitches) of the previous row, work 2 buttonhole stitches, throughout the row. Secure the thread, and space by overcasting along the braid for the next row.

This filling is also referred to as: Double net stitch, Double Brussels stitch, 2nd lace stitch and Point de Sorrento in other needlelace books.

Net

Work in the same manner as for Double knot, but work single buttonhole stitches instead of pairs.

This filling is also known as Single net stitch, Single Brussels, Point de Bruxelles and Tulle stitch.

PHOTOGRAPH 48 *Net*

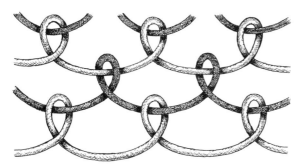

DRAWING 13 *Net*

Net and bar

Even stitches and row spacing are important. The first 3 rows are like Net filling

Foundation row: (*right to left*). Work single buttonhole stitches with a loop between each stitch, throughout the row.**

Space by overcasting along pinloop edge of braid.

1st row: (*left to right*). Into each loop of the previous row work a single buttonhole stitch.

Space by overcasting along pinloop edge of braid.

2nd row: (*right to left*). As 1st row. Directly beneath the last row (i.e. no spacing) take 2 single thread cords i.e. a single left to right and then a single right to left, securing the thread into the same braid pinloop.

Space by overcasting along pinloop edge of braid.

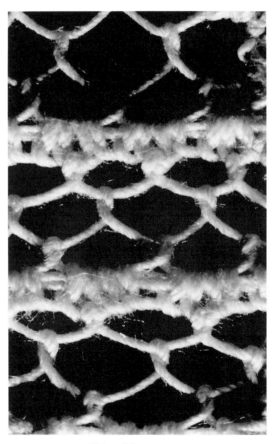

PHOTOGRAPH 49 *Net and bar*

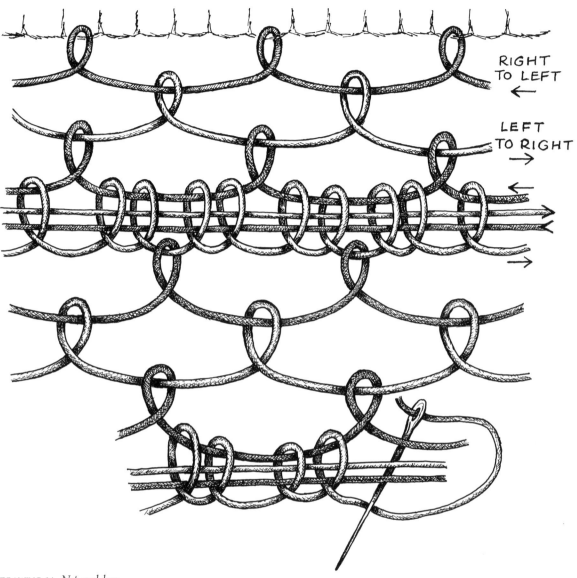

DRAWING 14 *Net and bar*

3rd row (the bar): (*left to right*). Work a row of close buttonhole stitches into the loops of the previous row, incorporating the 2 cords. Each loop should contain the same number (usually 4 or 6) of stitches.

Space by overcasting along pinloop edge of braid.

4th row: (*right to left*). Make a single buttonhole stitch into the centre loop between the blocks of stitches of the previous bar row

Repeat from **

Butterfly

Consists of 5 stitches, decreasing 1 stitch from each triangle per row. The spacing and evenness of stitches is important.

Foundation row: work a single buttonhole stitch into the braid pinloops with a loop between each stitch. The loop should be long enough to take 5 stitches of the 1st row.

1st row: into each loop work 5 buttonhole stitches, with a short loop between each group of stitches.

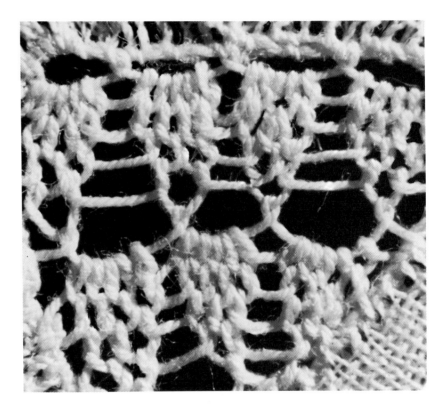

PHOTOGRAPH 50A *Butterfly*

2nd row: work 4 buttonhole stitches into the 4 loops between the 5 stitches of the 1st row.

3rd row: work 3 buttonhole stitches into the 3 loops between the 4 stitches of the 2nd row.

4th row: work 2 buttonhole stitches into the 2 loops between the 3 stitches of the 3rd row.

5th row: work 1 buttonhole stitch with the loops between each stitch longer, to take the 5 stitches for the 1st repeat row.

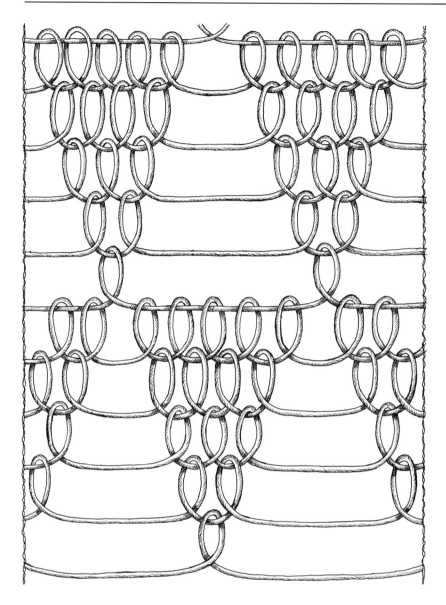

DRAWING 15 *Butterfly*

Note: Loops between the groups of stitches get longer as the stitches reduce in number. When there is not enough room for a complete butterfly, working an odd stitch or 2 (depending on the space to be filled) at either or both sides, may avoid unsightly gaps.

Butterfly is also referred to in other lace books as Pyramids, Point de Bruxelles, Tenth stitch and Fan stitch and it can be made with 8 stitches for the first block, reducing to 1 stitch.

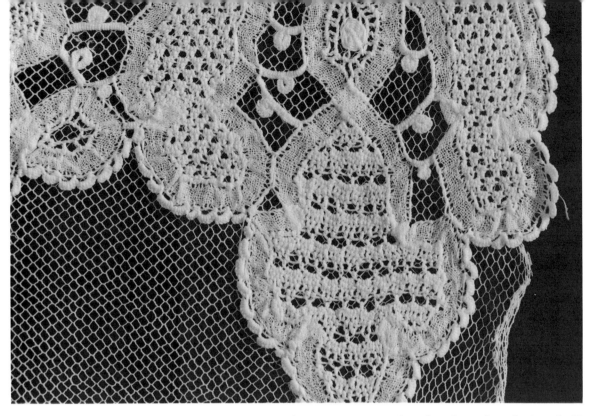

PHOTOGRAPH 50B *Butterfly variation seen on either side and just above the Butterfly filling (bottom centre)*

Butterfly variation

PHOTOGRAPH 50B shows Butterfly filling bottom-centre with Butterfly variation on either side just above. The photograph also clearly shows Rib bars, Work around, Flat cutwork and the purl edging.

Commence: (*right to left*). With single buttonhole stitches evenly spread and a short loop between each stitch. (Each loop to take 3 stitches in the 1st row.)

Space by overcasting along into the next pinloop of the braid, and between each row.

1st row: (*left to right*). Into each loop work 3 buttonhole stitches.

2nd row: (*right to left*). At the base and between the 3 stitches of the previous row, work a buttonhole stitch into each of 2 loops (close together) with a loop between each pair of stitches, to take 3 stitches in the 3rd row.

3rd row: (*left to right*). Work 3 buttonhole stitches over each loop, between the pairs of stitches of the previous row.

Repeat 2nd and 3rd rows.

Holey

This consists of blocks of 4 stitches under one another, in the 2 repeat rows.

Commence: (*right to left*). Work single buttonhole stitches with long and short loops alternately between each stitch. The long loops to take 4 stitches and the short loop to take 1 stitch in the 1st row.

Space by overcasting along the edge of the braid, between each row.

1st row Work 4 buttonhole stitches into the longer loops and 1 buttonhole stitch into the short loop, with a short loop either side of the single buttonhole stitch for the next row.

2nd row: Work a single buttonhole stitch into each of the small loops on either side of the single stitch of the 1st row, leaving a long loop under the block of 4 stitches, and a short loop for the single stitch in the next row.

This stitch is also referred to as One and Five stitch and Point Brabacon, with 6 stitches rather than 4.

PHOTOGRAPH 51 *Holey*

DRAWING 16 *Holey*

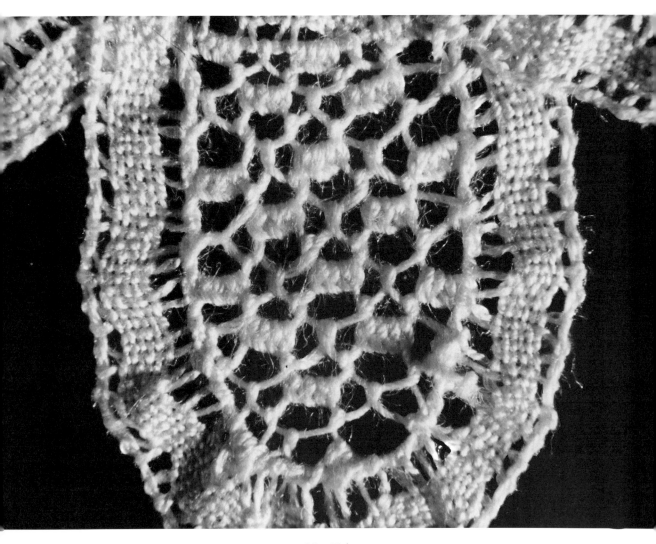

PHOTOGRAPH 52 *New Holey*

New Holey

Similar to Holey. Remember to space between each row by overcasting along the pinloop edge of the braid.

Commence: (*right to left*). Work single buttonhole stitches along the width of the braid, with long and short loops between each stitch. The long loops to take 4 stitches and the short loop a single stitch.

1st row: (*left to right*). Into each long loop work 4 buttonhole stitches and 1 stitch into alternate short loops.

2nd row: (*right to left*). Work a single buttonhole stitch over the loop either side of the block of 4 stitches in the previous row.

3rd row: (*left to right*). Work a repeat of the 1st row with the single buttonhole stitch being under the block of 4 stitches of the 1st row.

4th row: Repeat 2nd row.

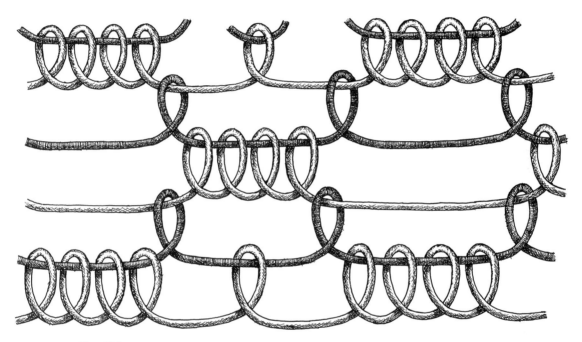

DRAWING 17 *New Holey*

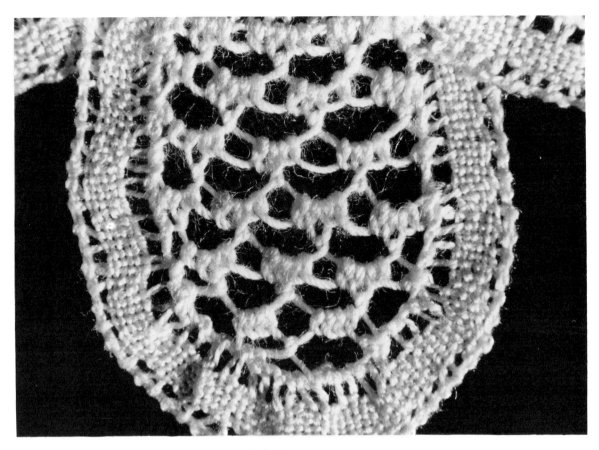

PHOTOGRAPH 53 *Jessie*

Jessie

Consists of two repeat rows.

Commence: (*right to left*). Work single buttonhole stitches evenly spaced, with fairly taut loops between each stitch. Each loop to take a block of 4 buttonhole stitches in the 1st row.

Space by overcasting along to the next pinloop of the braid, and between each row.

1st row: (*left to right*). Work 4 buttonhole stitches into each loop.

2nd row: (*right to left*). Work a single buttonhole stitch at the base and over the centre loop, between each block of 4 stitches. Make the loop between each stitch fairly taut to take the 4 stitches in the 1st repeat row.

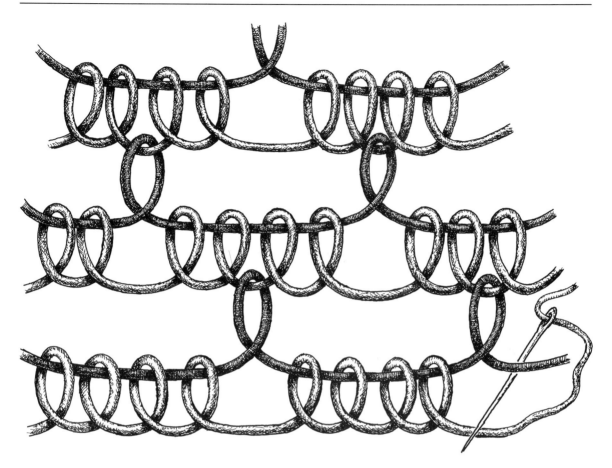

DRAWING 18 *Jessie*

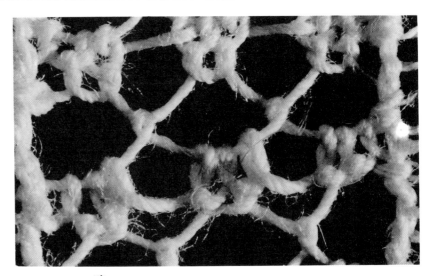

PHOTOGRAPH 54 *Eliza*

Eliza

Similar to Butterfly variation with the 3rd row of single stitches worked over the long loops between the *pairs* of stitches, and not between the two stitches.

Commence: Make single buttonhole stitches, evenly spaced, with fairly short loops between each stitch. Each loop to take 3 stitches in the 1st row.

Space by overcasting along into the next pinloop of the braid, and between each row.

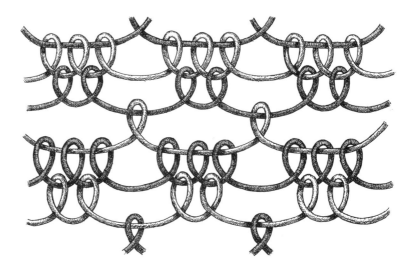

DRAWING 19 *Eliza*

1st row: Work 3 buttonhole stitches into each loop.

2nd row: At the base, between the 3 stitches of the previous row work a buttonhole stitch into each of the 2 loops, (close together).

3rd row: Work a single buttonhole stitch into the loop between the *pairs* of stitches of the 2nd row, with a loop between each stitch, to take 3 stitches of the 1st repeat row.

Repeat these 3 rows.

Charlotte

One of the many Point de Venise stitches and a very attractive filling when stitches are evenly worked and spaced. It is also known as Shell.

Commence: (*right to left*). Make single buttonhole stitches with fairly taut loops between each stitch. Each loop to take 3 stitches in the 1st row.**

Space by overcasting along braid pinloop edge between the rows.

PHOTOGRAPH 55 *Charlotte*

1st row: (*left to right*). Work 3 buttonhole stitches into each loop, working a 4th buttonhole locking stitch *sideways* across the bottom of these 3 stitches, thus forming a fan shape. (The 4th stitch being at the base in the loop immediately in front of the 1st of the 3 stitches.)

Note: Remember to keep the thread under your left-hand thumb until the 4th sideways locking stitch is almost pulled tight.

Space by overcasting along braid.

2nd row: (*right to left*). Work a single buttonhole stitch between each fan-shaped block of 3 stitches, with a fairly taut loop between each stitch.

Repeat from **.

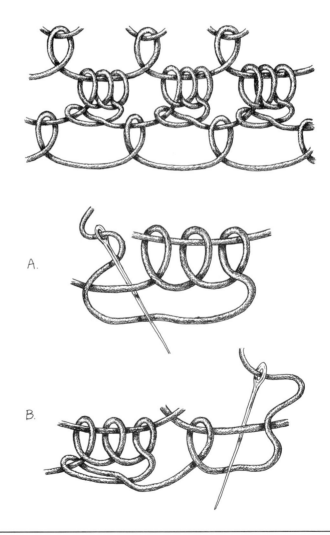

A.

B.

DRAWING 20 *Charlotte*

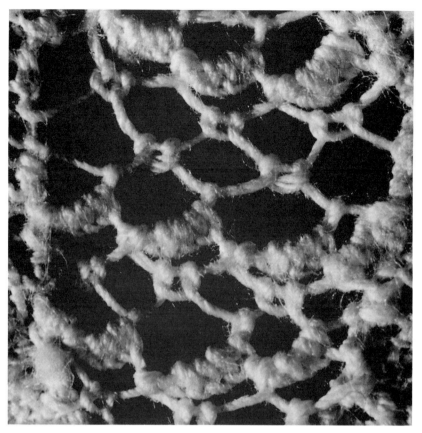

PHOTOGRAPH 56 *Rose's*

Rose's

This filling requires a little practise to achieve a good tension. Remember to space between the rows by overcasting along the edge of the braid. The 4th row is worked like the Branscombe Purl edging.

1st row: (*left to right*). Work along the width of the braid, spacing evenly. Make 2 buttonhole stitches close together with a *loose* loop between each pair of stitches.

2nd row: (*right to left*). Into each loop of the 1st row, make 2 buttonhole stitches close together with a loose loop between each pair of stitches (like the 1st row).

3rd row: work a Purl (like the purl edging) into every loop of 2nd row. Secure thread into left-hand braid, and work a single buttonhole stitch into the first loop (the foundation loop). Holding the thread firmly under left-hand thumb, work 5 buttonhole stitches from left to right, over the foundation loop. Repeat throughout the row.

4th row: work a *single* buttonhole stitch between each purl, keeping the loops between each stitch fairly taut.

This filling is similar to one of the Point de Venise stitches called Side and Net stitch, but has more net rows.

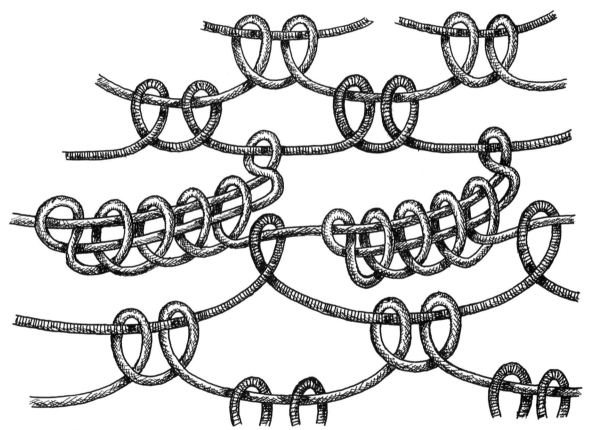

DRAWING 21 *Rose's*

Auntie Somers' Four-Bar

Blocks of 4 buttonhole stitches, with a loop between each to take the 4 buttonhole stitches in the repeat rows.

1st row: work 4 close buttonhole stitches into pinloop edge of braid then a loop to take 4 stitches in the next row. Repeat to end of row.

Space by overcasting along pinloop edge of braid.

2nd and repeat rows: into each loop of the previous row, work 4 buttonhole stitches, with a loop between each block of 4 stitches.

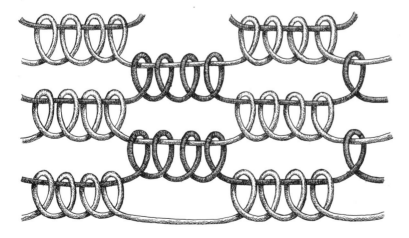

DRAWING 22 *Auntie Somers' Four-bar*

Zigzag

Similar to Four Bar. Use for narrow spaces and insertions.

Secure the thread into right-hand corner, and overcast along the width of the braid to centre.

Foundation row: make a single thread half bar-loop by securing the thread, spaced a little along the left side of the braid.

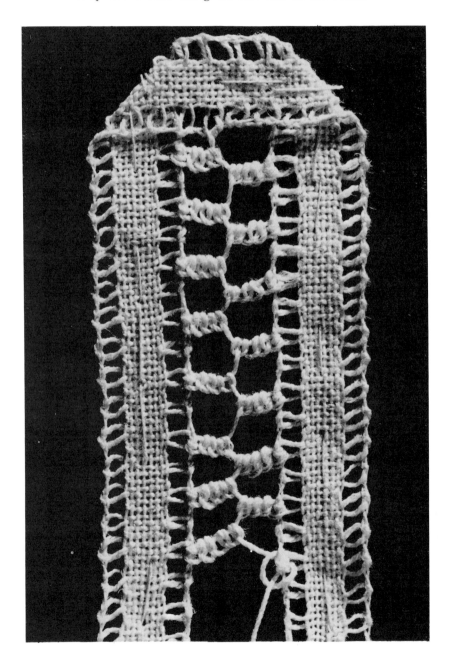

PHOTOGRAPH 58A *Zigzag*

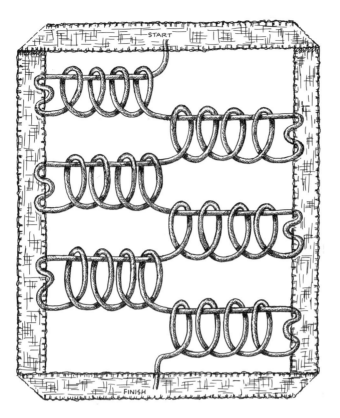

1st row: over this loop work 4 buttonhole stitches to centre. Make a single thread half bar-loop securing thread on the right-hand side of the braid, spaced just below the previous block of stitches.

2nd row: over this loop work 4 buttonhole stitches towards the centre.

Note: When working this filling in a circle: commence by making a single thread bar-loop from one side to the other between the two braid edges.

Right to left: work a block of 4 buttonhole stitches to reach halfway along this bar-loop. The other half of this bar-loop is used to work a block of 4 buttonhole stitches at the finish.

This is also referred to in other needle laces as Half-Bar insertion and Broken Bars.

PHOTOGRAPH 58B *Detail of Zigzag showing the stitches worked to fill space*

73

PHOTOGRAPH 59 *Wheatsheaf. (Also see* PHOTOGRAPH 28.*)*

Wheatsheaf

This makes an attractive insertion for a circle, or between two narrow straight braids.

Evenness and spacing of the bars is important and the middle of the 3 bars should be fairly taut, with the other 2 slightly less taut to allow for anchoring the 3 bars together.

Space evenly either side of the middle bar.

Secure thread into right-hand braid.

First bar: take a single thread, securing thread into left-hand braid.

Coil (twist) needle with thread over the bar, 3 or more times (depending on the width of bar) and secure thread into the same braid pinloop of the bar.

Overcast along the next 2 braid pinloops (allowing 1 pinloop space between bars).

2nd bar: as 1st bar. Overcast along 2 braid pinloops.

3rd bar: repeat, as for 1st bar, but coil thread just to the centre of the bar. Work two buttonhole stitches over the 3 bars, anchoring them together. Coil thread over other half of 3rd bar securing into same braid pinloop of bar.

Overcast along into the *next* braid pinloop, for the 1st bar of the next group.

Note: The 3rd bar of the last group and the 1st bar of the next group are close together, allowing a fraction more space either side of 2nd (middle) bar.

In other needlelaces this is referred to as Cluster insertion.

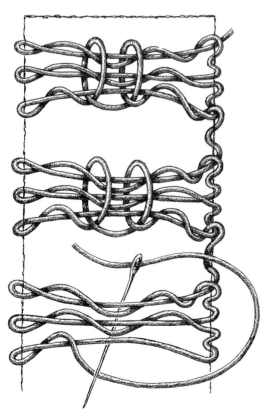

DRAWING 24 *Wheatsheaf*

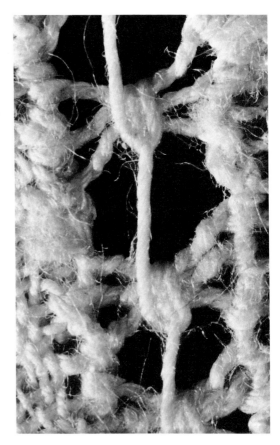

PHOTOGRAPH 60B *Detail of Olive's Wheatsheaf*

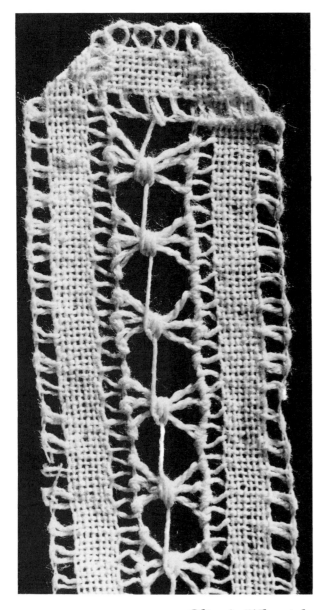

PHOTOGRAPH 60A *Olive's Wheatsheaf*

Olive's Wheatsheaf

This is similar to Wheatsheaf but requires making and even spacing of all the bars throughout the narrow space, between two braids first.

Remember to count the bars, for groups of 3 to be anchored together. Make the 3rd bar of the last group, and the 1st bar of the next group closer together, with a fraction more space either side of the 2nd (middle) bar.

2nd stage: anchor the groups of three bars together with 3 buttonhole stitches, with the thread continuous from one group of 3 bars to the next.

Make 3 buttonhole stitches over 3 bars, from left to right, alternating right to left over the next group of 3 bars.

Note: When working this insertion in a circle, make all the twisted bars of the insertion first, but on the *last* bar only, coil (twist) the thread halfway along the bar, and use the same thread to anchor the groups of 3 bars together around the circle.

Finish by coiling the thread along the second half of the last bar and securing into the braid.

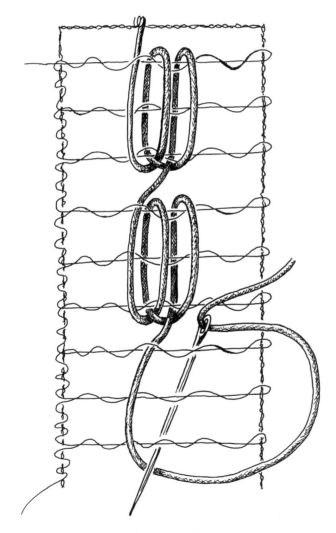

DRAWING 25 *Olive's Wheatsheaf*

Nibs

The way in which the Nib (picot) is made in the centre of the bar is believed to be unique to Branscombe Point lace, and helps with identification.

It can be used to fill any space, as a narrow filling or an insertion.

Foundation: secure thread into right-hand braid.

1st stage: between 2 braid edges, and into the *same* braid pinloops each side: make 3 single-thread bars.

2nd stage: over these 3 threads, from left to right, work close buttonhole stitches to the centre.

3rd stage: make a single buttonhole stitch on the far right-hand side (against the braid) at **A**, this being the foundation loop for the Nib.

Keep this stitch-loop fairly taut

Over this stitch-loop, from left to right, work 5 tight buttonhole stitches, holding the thread taut under your left-hand thumb, and do not release it until the first stitch is almost pulled into position. (The first stitch will be worked over 1 thread of the loop, with the following 4 stitches worked over two threads.)

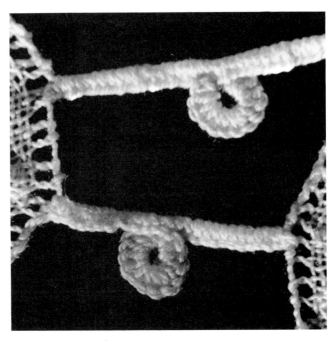

PHOTOGRAPH 61 *Nibs*

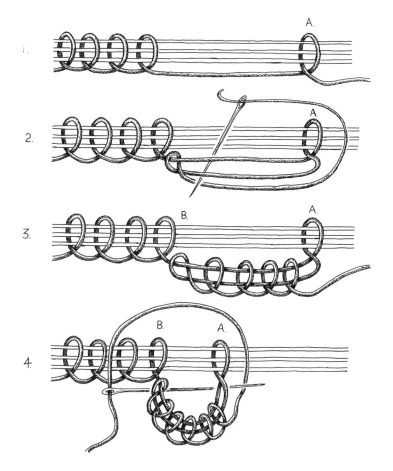

DRAWING 26 *Nibs*

4th stage: slide stitch **A** to centre **B**. Lock **A** and **B** together by working 2 tight buttonhole stitches across the Nib, again keeping the thread under your left-hand thumb until the stitches are almost pulled tight into position.

5th stage: complete the other half of the bar with close buttonhole stitches, from the centre to the right-hand edge of braid. Fasten thread.

Note: Space by overcasting along the edge of the right-hand braid. The number of tight buttonhole stitches required to form the Nib depends on the length of the foundation loops and on the working thread. With a finer thread 7 stitches may be required.

PHOTOGRAPH 62 *Purling: the decorative edging*

Purling

This is the traditional attractive edge one looks for when identifying Branscombe Point Lace. It is added to the outer edge of a finished article.

1st stage: from left to right make a foundation loop, by working a buttonhole stitch from 1 braid pinloop to the next, keeping the stitch-loop fairly taut.

2nd stage: work 5 buttonhole stitches into the foundation loop, from left to right, holding the thread back, and keeping it taut under the left-hand thumb. Do not release it until the 1st stitch is nearly pulled into position.

Note: The 1st stitch will be over the single thread of the loop, with the following 4 stitches worked over two threads.

3rd stage: with *no* spacing between the purls, make the next foundation loop into the next braid pinloop.

Having to miss a braid pinloop, to make room for the purls to lie flat, indicates the thread being used is too thick.

This type of Purl or Picot is found on Youghal lace and is also one of several edgings used in Venetian lace.

DRAWING 27 *Purling*

Ribbed Cutwork

This is useful and attractive for the centre of small circles and spaces. It requires an even number of fairly taut spokes, or twisted bars (Branscombe lacemakers call these 'legs').

1st stage: bring your needle up through the braid pinloop **A**. Make a single thread bar from **A** to **B**, securing with a tight buttonhole stitch. Coil the thread over the bar several times (depending on the length of the bar), from **B** to the centre.

PHOTOGRAPH 63A *Ribbed Cutwork: the reverse, i.e. working side*

PHOTOGRAPH 63B *Ribbed Cutwork: the right side*

Secure thread in the centre with a tight buttonhole stitch.

2nd stage: make a single thread bar by bringing the needle up through the braid pinloop at **C**. Secure with a tight buttonhole stitch.

3rd stage: **once more, coil back to centre, and secure with another single, tight, buttonhole stitch. Bring the needle up through the braid pinloop at **D**.

Repeat from ** until the required *even* number of spokes are made.

Note: Spoke **A** will remain a single-thread spoke, to denote the start and finish.

From the centre, working clockwise, backstitch over and around every spoke (as shown in the illustration) to give the raised effect on the right side.

Finish on spoke **A**, by coiling the thread out to the braid and fastening off.

Ribbed Cutwork is also known as: Rosette in Raised Point d'Angleterre, Spinning Wheel, Web, Cobwebs, Spider and Sorrento Wheels in other needlelaces and embroidery.

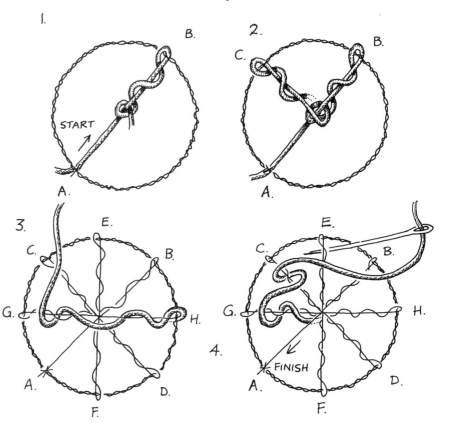

DRAWING 28 *Ribbed Cutwork*

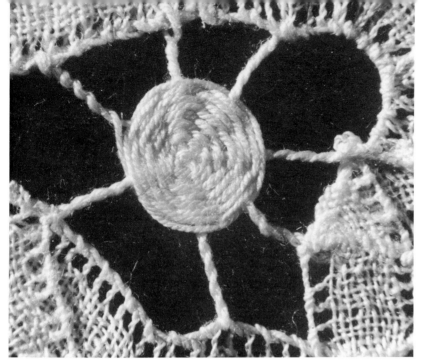

Flat Cutwork

As its name suggests, this does not create a raised effect.

The end result is an *uneven* number of spokes, but made in the same way as for the Ribbed Cutwork.

After enough spokes are made to fill the area (*see* Ribbed Cutwork), working from the centre, weave the needle and thread under one spoke and over the next, (i.e. darning method) until the filling is the required size.

Finish as for Ribbed Cutwork.

This is also referred to as: Cobwebs, Spider and Sorrento Wheels in other needlelaces and embroidery.

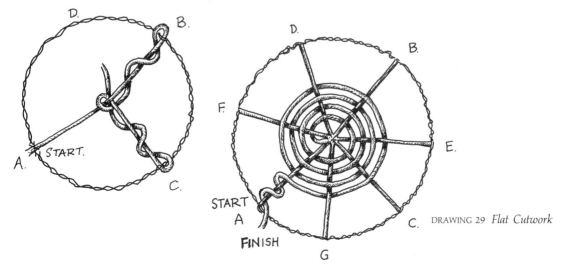

DRAWING 29 *Flat Cutwork*

83

Work Around

Some prefer to work this from left to right, making a circle of buttonhole stitches with an extra twist. The method described here is the Branscombe way, which helps to keep a good tension.

1st round: *(right to left)*. Fasten thread on edge of one braid pinloop, take needle up through next braid pinloop to the left. Wrap long end of thread from the eye of the needle around the point of the needle, twice in a clockwise direction. Pull the needle through, creating a double-twisted buttonhole stitch.

Space loops evenly around the circle.

2nd round: overcast into each loop and pull the thread taut.

These 2 rows are repeated in larger holes to fill the space.

PHOTOGRAPH 65 *Work Around*

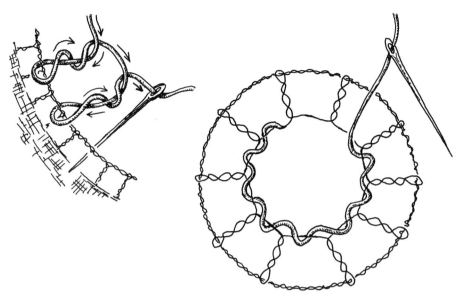

DRAWING 30 *Work Around*

Note: at the start there will be a single thread with no twists.

Finish by coiling the needle and thread over last loop to form twists, and fasten into braid.

This is also referred to as: Point d'Espagne and Open Wheels.

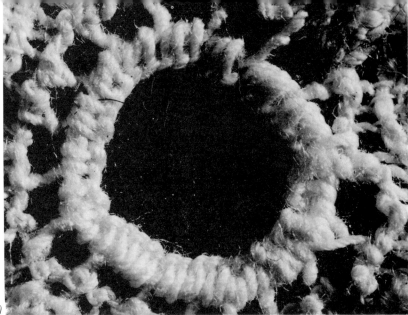

PHOTOGRAPH 66 *Buttonhole circle in Work Around.*
(Also see PHOTOGRAPHS 40 *and* 41.)

Buttonhole Circle in Work Around

After completing the first 2 rounds of Work Around work a circle of close buttonhole stitches around the centre. Also see PHOTOGRAPHS 38, 39A and 39B.

Treble Cluster

This is found in Branscombe Point lace, as the centre of Work Around, see PHOTOGRAPH 10. You can see it used as an insertion in PHOTOGRAPH 68. From DIAGRAM 31 you can see that it consists of 3 twisted bars.

PHOTOGRAPH 67 *Treble Cluster.*
(Also see PHOTOGRAPH 10.)

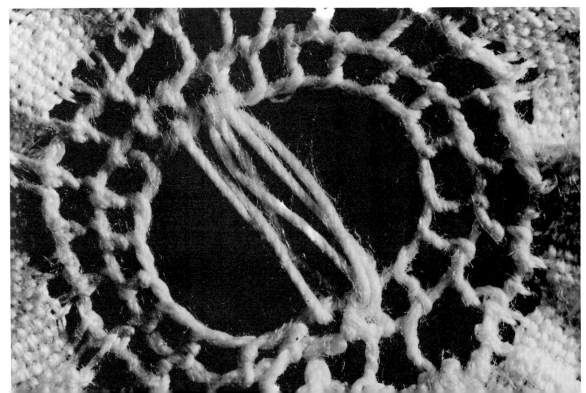

PHOTOGRAPH 68 *Treble insertion*

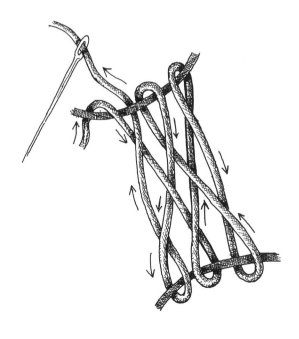

DRAWING 31 *Treble Cluster*

Leadwork

This is not often found in Branscombe Point lace as the Treble Cluster is much easier to make. It is woven exactly like the Honiton bobbin-lace leadworks, but using a needle (*see* PHOTOGRAPH 69). DRAWING 32 illustrates the weaving method.

PHOTOGRAPH 69 *Leadwork centre in Work Around*

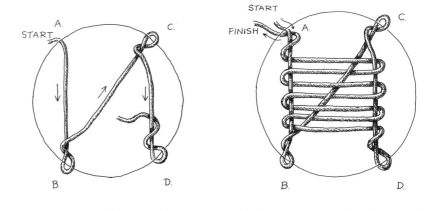

DRAWING 32 *Leadwork*

Lozenge

This is often called Leadwork, but it is easier to make. Spacing the twisted bars is important, when working this as an insertion.

1st stage: make 3 bars as for Wheatsheaf. First make a single-thread bar from braid edge **A** to braid edge **B**. Secure the thread and coil it over the bar back to **A**. Make a 2nd and 3rd bar as the 1st.

2nd stage: coil the thread once or twice back to the beginning of the first bar. Weave the lozenge taking the thread over and under the 3 foundation bars (*see* illustration).

After weaving the lozenge, finish coiling the thread along this bar, and secure it into the braid edge.

Repeat.

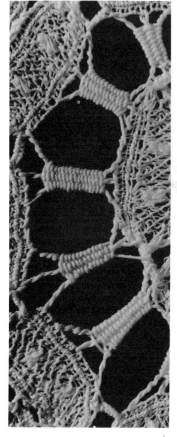

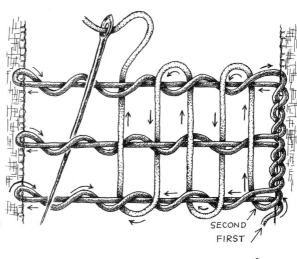

DRAWING 33 *Lozenge*

PHOTOGRAPH 70 *Lozenge. A detail from* PHOTOGRAPH 32

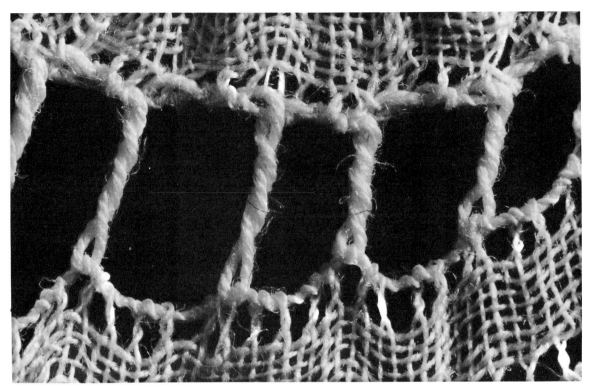

PHOTOGRAPH 71 *Twisted Bar insertion*

Twisted Bar insertion

This is a simple insertion found in poor-quality Branscombe Point.

The bars are worked as the bars in Ladder Trail, coiling the thread several times over the single-thread foundation bar.

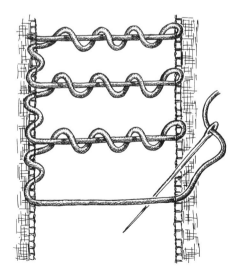

DRAWING 34 *Twisted Bar insertion*

Cross-bar insertion

Evenness in spacing the bars is important.

1st stage: a single taut thread is carried diagonally from side to side of the narrow space, securing the thread into the pinloop edges of the braids. On reaching the end of the space, double back, coiling over each taut bar-loop, again securing thread into the braids each side.

2nd stage: connect a new thread and repeat, starting on the opposite side of the narrow space.

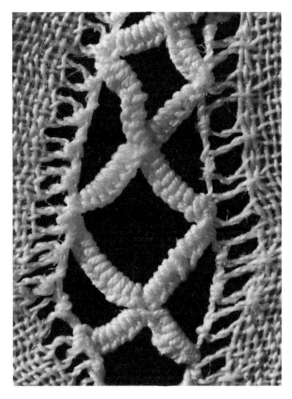

PHOTOGRAPH 72 *Cross-bar insertion*

This completes the cross-over foundation bars.

3rd stage: working diagonally again, over the foundation bars, make close buttonhole stitches, leaving a short space where the foundation bars cross over.

4th stage: the cross-over space will be filled with buttonhole stitches (on crossing over) when working diagonally the other way (2nd time).

I.

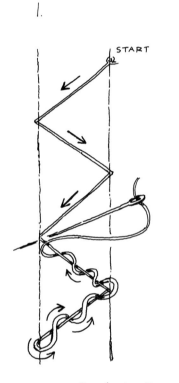

DRAWING 35 *Cross-bar insertion*

2.

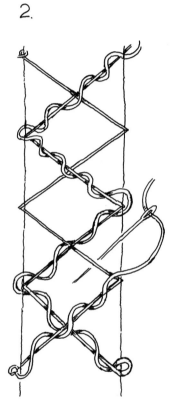

3.

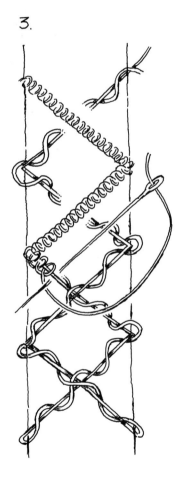

Ladder Trail insertion

Spacing the bars is important.

The bars: secure the thread into the right-hand braid. Make a single-thread bar, securing the thread into the left-hand braid.

Coil (twist) the thread over the bar and secure back into the right-hand braid.

Space by overcasting along the pinloop edge of the braid.

Repeat until all the bars have been made, then fasten off thread.

Connect a new thread into the braid above the top bar (centre left-side).

**Carry a single thread down to left-hand side of the bar.

Left to right: over the bar, work 5, 6 or 7 buttonhole stitches, to the right-hand side of the bar.

Repeat from ** until all the bars have been worked.

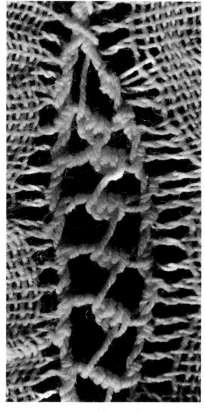

PHOTOGRAPH 73 *Ladder Trail insertion*

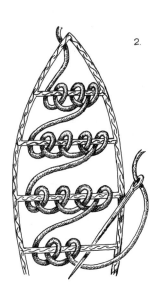

DRAWING 36 *Ladder Trail insertion*

Purl filling

The purls are made as Purling for the outer edge of a finished article – a 2-row repeat.

Foundation row: (*left to right*). Make Purls (*see* DRAWING 27) across the width of the braid.

1st row: (*right to left*). Work a single buttonhole stitch between each Purl, throughout the row, with a loop between each stitch (the loop to take a Purl in the next row).

Space by overcasting along the side of the braid.

2nd row: (*left to right*). On to each loop of the previous row, make (the foundation stitch for) a Purl.

Repeat these 2 rows.

PHOTOGRAPH 74 *Purl Filling*

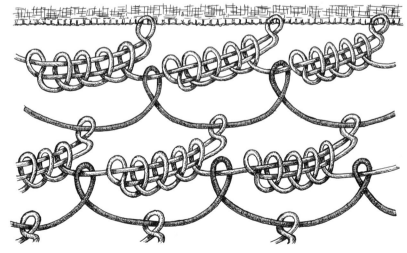

DRAWING 37 *Purl filling*

PHOTOGRAPH 75 *Treble Stitch,
worked like Double knot
but with three buttonhole stitches
instead of two*

Treble stitch

This is similar to Double Knot, but consists of 3 stitches instead of 2.

1st row: work 3 buttonhole stitches close together, with a loop between each block of stitches to take 3 stitches in the next row.

Space between rows by overcasting along the side of the braid.

2nd and repeat rows: work 3 buttonhole stitches over each loop of the previous row, again with a loop between each block of 3 stitches to take 3 stitches in the next row.

Space as before.

This filling is also known as Triple stitch and Third Lace stitch.

DRAWING 38 *Treble stitch*

Little Jessie's

This is found in Branscombe lace.

Foundation row: (*left to right*). Make a single buttonhole stitch into each of 2 braid pinloops. Miss the next braid pinloop. Repeat to end of row, along the width of braid. Secure thread.

Space by overcasting along into the next braid pinloop.

1st row: (*right to left*). Over the loops, between each pair of stitches, work 1 buttonhole stitch with a loop between each stitch, throughout the row. Secure the thread.

Space by overcasting along into the next braid pinloop.

2nd row: (*left to right*) Over the loops, between each single stitch of the previous row, work 2 buttonhole stitches.

Space by overcasting along into the next braid pinloop.

Repeat 1st and 2nd rows, to fill the space between the braids.

PHOTOGRAPH 76 *Little Jessie's*

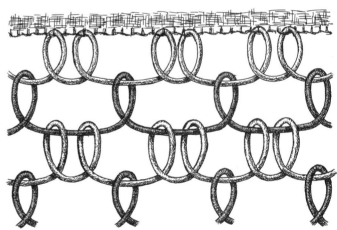

DRAWING 39 *Little Jessie's*

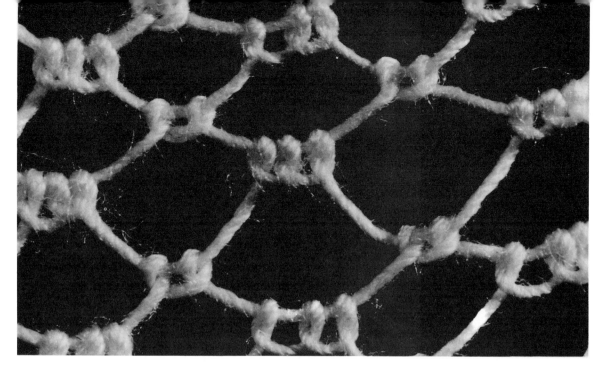

New Eliza's

Foundation row: (*left to right*). Evenly space groups of 3 buttonhole stitches along the whole length of the braid leaving a loop to take 2 stitches in the next row.

Space between 2 rows by overcasting along the side of the braid.

1st row: (*right to left*). Work 2 buttonhole stitches over the loops of the previous row.

Space.

2nd row: (*left to right*). Work 3 buttonhole stitches over each loop between the pairs of stitches in the 1st row.

Repeat the 1st and 2nd rows.

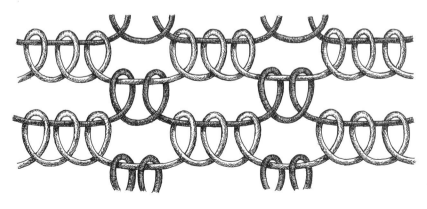

DRAWING 40 *New Eliza's*

Four and three stitch

Four and three stitch is found in Honiton Point lace.

Foundation row: (*left to right*). Make 4 buttonhole stitches, fairly close together, with a loop between each block of 4 stitches, along the width of the braid.

**Space* by overcasting along the pinloop edge of the braid.

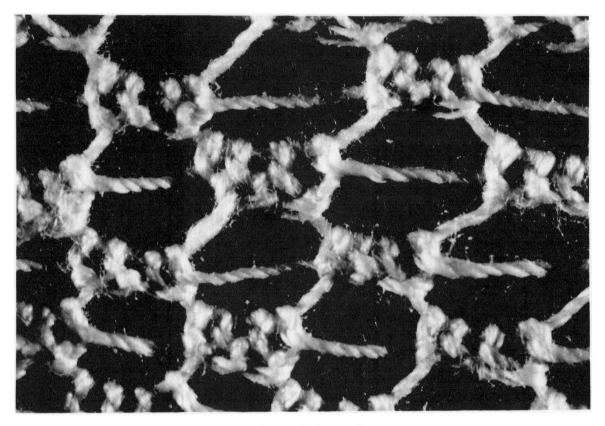

PHOTOGRAPH 78 *Four and Three stitch*

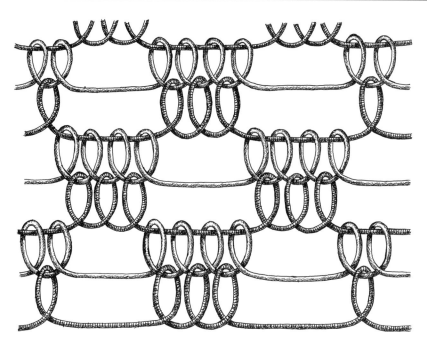

DRAWING 41 *Four and Three
Stitch (or Combination stitch)*

1st row: (*right to left*). Make a single buttonhole stitch over each tiny loop (3) between each loop of the block of 4 stitches with a loop between each block of 3 stitches.

Space by overcasting along the pinloop edge of the braid.

2nd row: (*left to right*). Over each loop between the blocks of 3 stitches in the previous row, work 4 buttonhole stitches.

Repeat from ** to fill the space between braids.

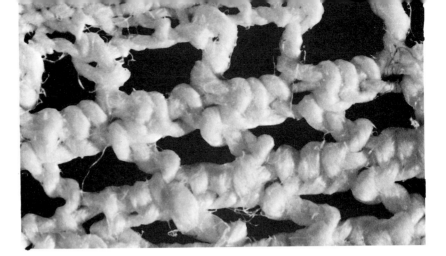

PHOTOGRAPH 79 *Church stitch*

Church stitch

The spaces between rows and stitches should be square.

Foundation row: (*right to left*). Make a single buttonhole stitch with an extra twist, spaced evenly along the row, with a loop between each stitch, to take 3 stitches in the next row.

Space by overcasting along the braid pinloop edge (approx. 2 pinloops).

1st row: (*left to right*). Over each loop of the previous row work 3 buttonhole stitches, with a short loop between each block of 3 stitches.

Space between the rows by overcasting along the braid pinloops.

2nd row: (*right to left*). Into each short loop between the blocks of 3 stitches, work a single buttonhole stitch with an extra twist.

Repeat 1st and 2nd rows.

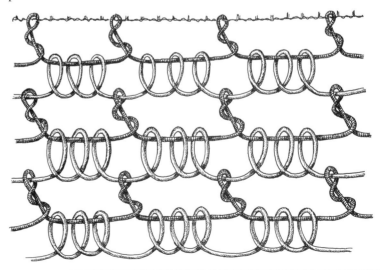

DRAWING 42 *Church stitch*

Church stitch variation

Foundation row: (*right to left*). Work 3 single buttonhole stitches with an extra twist in each stitch, with short loops between each stitch (2 short loops). Make a loop to take 4 stitches in the next row between each block of 3 stitches.

Space by overcasting along the braid pinloops (approx. 2 pinloops).

1st row: (*left to right*). *Make 4 buttonhole stitches over the long loop of the previous row. Make a short loop (to take 1 stitch). Make a single buttonhole stitch over each of the 2 short loops in the previous row (between the 3 stitches with extra twists) with a short loop between these 2 stitches. Make a short loop.

Repeat from * throughout the row.

PHOTOGRAPH 80 *Church stitch variation*

2nd row: (*right to left*). **Directly below the 4 stitches in the previous row make a loop (to take 4 stitches). Make a single buttonhole stitch with an extra twist over each of the next 3 short loops. Repeat from ** throughout the row.

Space along the pinloop edge of the braid.

Note: where the space to be filled between the braids is irregular, or narrows, you may need to work 5 or 6 stitches instead of 4.

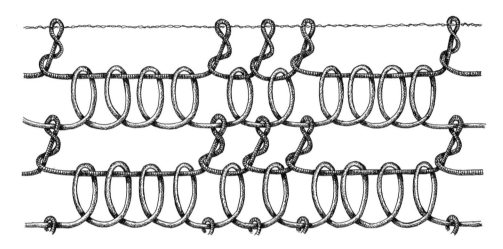

DRAWING 43 *Church stitch variation*

Shell stitch

Foundation row: (*right to left*). Into the braid pinloops work a row of single buttonhole stitches with a loop between each stitch (the loop to take 6 stitches in the next row).

Space by overcasting along the braid pinloop edge.

1st row: (*left to right*). Over each loop of the previous row work 6 buttonhole stitches.

Space by overcasting (approx. 2 pinloops) along edge of braid.

2nd row: (*right to left*). Work a single buttonhole stitch with an extra twist over the centre loop (between the block) of the 6 stitches in the previous row, with a loop between each stitch to take 6 stitches in the next, (i.e. 1st repeat) row.

Space.

Repeat 1st and 2nd rows.

There are variations to this filling stitch.

PHOTOGRAPH 81 *Shell stitch*

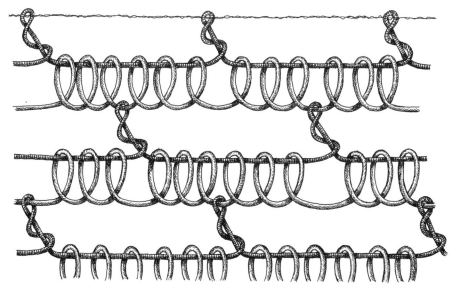

DRAWING 44 *Shell stitch*

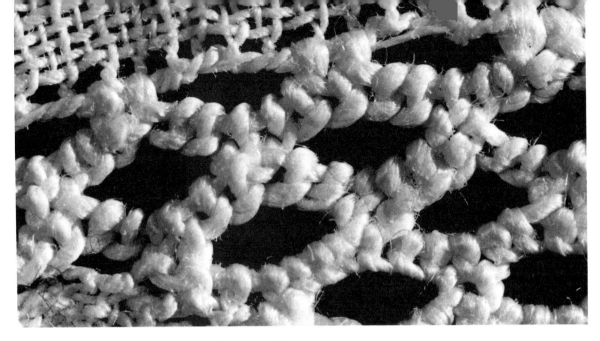

Scallop stitch

This is similar to Shell filling.

Foundation row: (*right to left*). Make 2 buttonhole stitches close together, with a long loop between each pair of stitches.

Space by overcasting along the pinloop edge of the braid.

1st row: (*left to right*). Into each loop of the previous row work 5 buttonhole stitches.

Space by overcasting along the pinloop edge of the braid.

2nd row: (*right to left*). Work a single buttonhole stitch over the loops each side of the middle (3rd) stitch of each block of 5 stitches of the 1st row.

Space by overcasting along the pinloop edge of the braid.

Repeat 1st and 2nd rows to fill the space between braids.

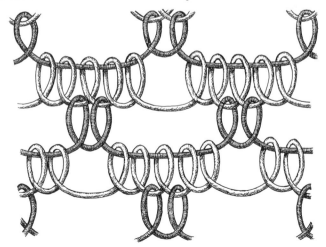

DRAWING 45 *Scallop stitch*

Diamond net

This is a very attractive filling, but practice is required to work it successfully as it is quite difficult to keep the blocks of stitches evenly spaced, and the loops between stitches must be all the same length. The blocks of stitches are diamond shape.

Foundation row: (*left to right*). Work along the width of the braid. Space with a long single-thread loop. * Work 5 buttonhole stitches fairly close together.

Space with a long single-thread loop.

Repeat from * throughout the row.

PHOTOGRAPH 83A *Diamond net, showing correct, even spacing*

PHOTOGRAPH 83B *Diamond net, shown here unevenly spaced, with too fine a thread for the braid. Very poor quality work*

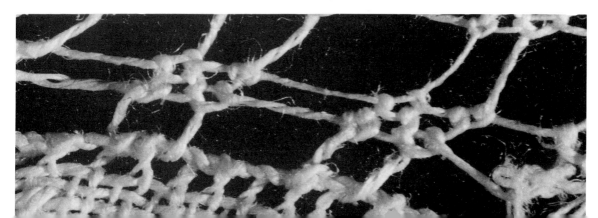

Space by overcasting along the pinloop edge of the braid (using the depth of the loop as a rough guide).

1st row: (*right to left*). Make a single buttonhole stitch over the loop on each side of the 3rd stitch of the block of 5 stitches in the previous row. Work 2 buttonhole stitches close together over the centre of each long loop of the previous row, holding the loop under your left-hand thumb. (These 2 stitches are the foundation pair for the block of 5 stitches in the next row.)

Note: The loop between each pair of stitches must be the same length as the depth of the loop in previous row.

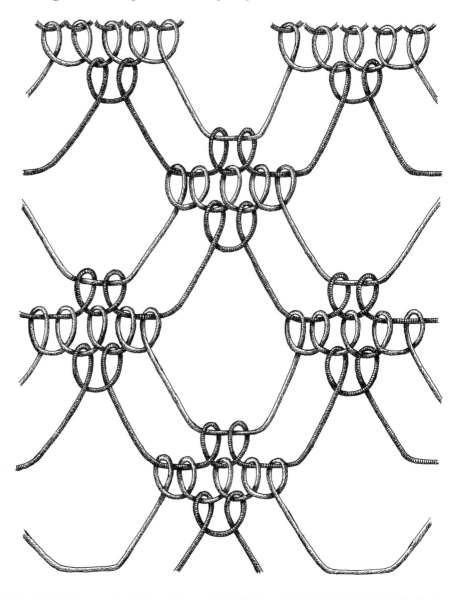

DRAWING 46 *Diamond net*

Space by overcasting into the *next* pinloop of the braid.

2nd row: (*left to right*). Make 2 close buttonhole stitches over the loops each side of the previous pair of stitches, with a single buttonhole stitch over the loop between the previous pair, thus giving a block of 5 stitches. Then work a long single-thread loop as in the foundation row.

Repeat the 1st and 2nd rows to complete the space between braids.

This stitch was one of many often referred to as Combination stitch.

Linen stitches

There are several variations to be found in Honiton Point lace but it is very rarely found in Branscombe Point lace.

Single linen stitch

This is worked exactly like Net filling, but with all the stitches very close together.

PHOTOGRAPH 84 *Single Linen stitch*

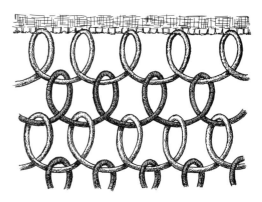

DRAWING 47 *Linen stitch*

Double linen stitch

This is worked in the same way as Double Knot filling, with each pair of stitches very close together.

Linen stitch with cord

Foundation row: (*left to right*). Work a row of even buttonhole stitches close together, as in Single linen stitch. Secure the thread into the pinloop edge of the braid.

* Directly below the row of stitches, take the thread (cord) from right to left, and anchor into the left-hand braid. Overcast into the next pinloop of braid edge.

Next row: (*left to right*). Work a single buttonhole stitch into each loop between the stitches of the foundation row, over and incorporating the cord.

Repeat from * to fill the space between braids.

PHOTOGRAPH 86 *Linen stitch with cord*

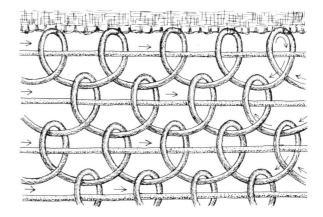

DRAWING 48 *Linen stitch with cord*

108

PHOTOGRAPH 87 *Linen stitch variations with cord, with a single buttonhole stitch*

Linen stitch variation with cord

This is often found in Branscombe Point lace. It is worked the same way as Linen stitch with cord, with spacing beween rows and stitches.

Foundation row: (*left to right*). Work single buttonhole stitches as in Net filling, with a short space and loop between each buttonhole stitch. Secure the thread into the pinloop of the braid. Overcast along the pinloop edge of the braid.

* (*Right to left.*) Take the thread (cord) and anchor it into the left-hand braid. Overcast along the pinloop edge of the braid.

Next row: (*left to right*). Work a single buttonhole stitch over each loop, between the stitches of the previous row of stitches, incorporating the cord.

Repeat from * to fill the space between braids.

Note: PHOTOGRAPH 87 shows a single buttonhole stitch; PHOTOGRAPH 88 shows a double buttonhole stitch.

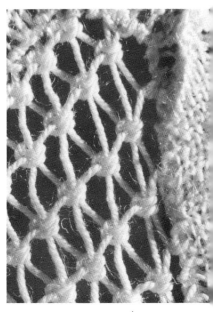

PHOTOGRAPH 88 *Linen stitch variations with cord, with a double buttonhole stitch*

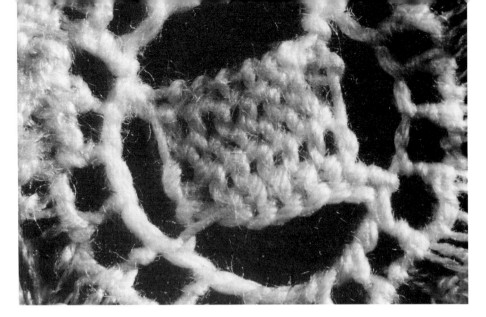

Linen stitch block in Work Around

This is a small square of Linen stitch in the centre of a Work Around, which is found in Branscombe Point.

Start from the position of having pulled the thread taut in the 2nd overcast round, of the Work Around.

Secure a single thread foundation square by working tight buttonhole stitches with an extra twist in 4 places.

Fill the square with Linen stitch, looping the thread around the foundation thread at the end of each row.

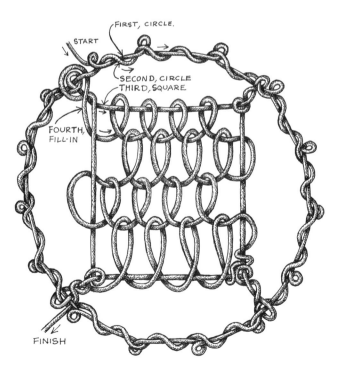

DRAWING 49 *Linen stitch block in Work Around*

Wavily stitch

This is very effective filling, seldom found in Branscombe Point lace.

The diagonal lines and evenness of the stitches require some practice to achieve a pleasing result.

The stitch consists of 3 buttonhole stitches with a taut loop between each block of 3 stitches. It is important that all the loops, between each group of 3 buttonhole stitches throughout the filling, are the same length.

Avoid unsightly gaps at the end of rows by working extra stitch(es) instead of a loop, before securing the thread into the braid.

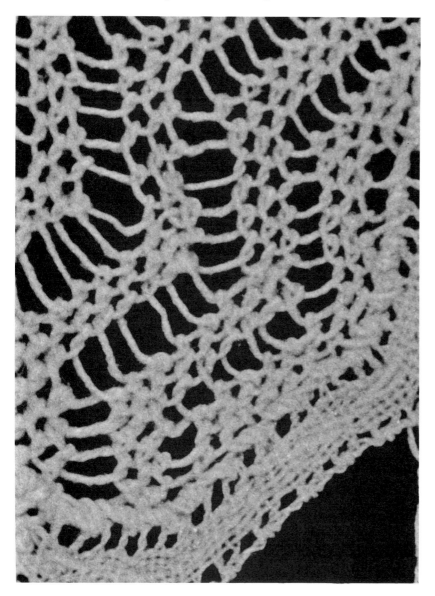

PHOTOGRAPH 90A *Wavily stitch*

PHOTOGRAPH 90B *Wavily stitch*

Diagonal lines, right to left: (*working left to right*). The first stitch of each block of 3 stitches is worked over the long loop to the left (i.e. before the 1st stitch) of the block of 3 stitches of the previous row.

(*Working right to left.*) The 1st stitch is worked over the short loop between the first 2 stitches of the block of the previous row.

Diagonal lines, left to right: (*working left to right*). The 1st stitch is worked over the short loop between the first 2 stitches of the block in the previous row.

(*Working right to left.*) The 1st stitch is worked over the long loop to the right of the 1st stitch of the block in the previous row.

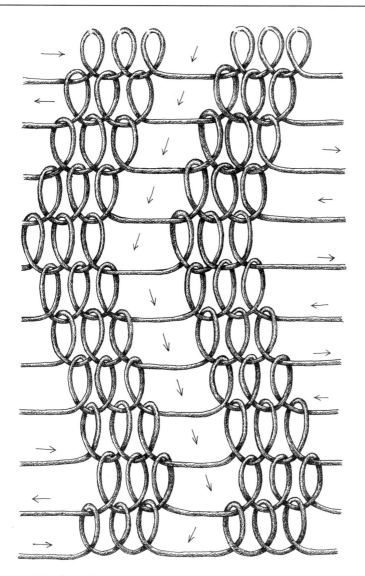

DRAWING 50 *Wavily stitch*

Wheels

This is a very effective filling and not so difficult as it appears. It can also be used as an insertion.

Make a single-thread bar from braid edge **A** across to the edge of braid at **B**. Secure the thread with a tight buttonhole stitch. Coil the thread over the bar back to **A**. Secure the thread.

Space by overcasting along the edge of the braid.

Continue making horizontal bars.

Vertical bars: take a single thread from **C** to **D**, making a tight buttonhole stitch at **X** to anchor the thread where the bars cross over.

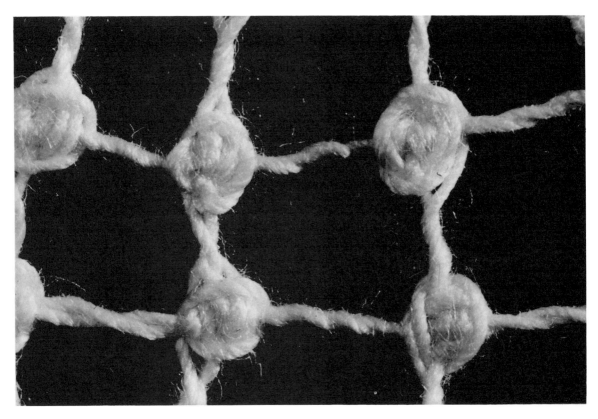

PHOTOGRAPH 91 *Wheels.* (Also see PHOTOGRAPH 10.)

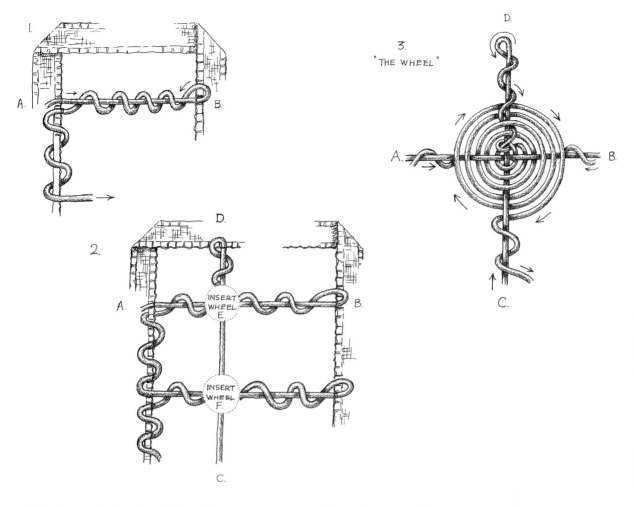

DRAWING 51 *Wheels*

Wheels: coil the thread from **D** to cross over at **E**, making a 2nd tight buttonhole stitch. Weave the needle over and under the 4 bars to make a wheel — **E**.

The wheel: for the *first two rounds* the thread passes *over* **D** and **C**, and *under* **B** and **A**.

3rd circle: the thread passes *between* the 2 threads of the coiled bar **D**, over **B**, under **C** and over **A**.

4th circle: pass the thread under **D** and **C**, over **B** and **A**.

5th circle: pass the thread under **D** and over **B**; at **C** coil the thread along the bar to the next cross-over at **F** and work another wheel.

Note: PHOTOGRAPH 10 shows a wheel in the centre of tiny circles. Spacing and keeping the foundation bars taut is important.

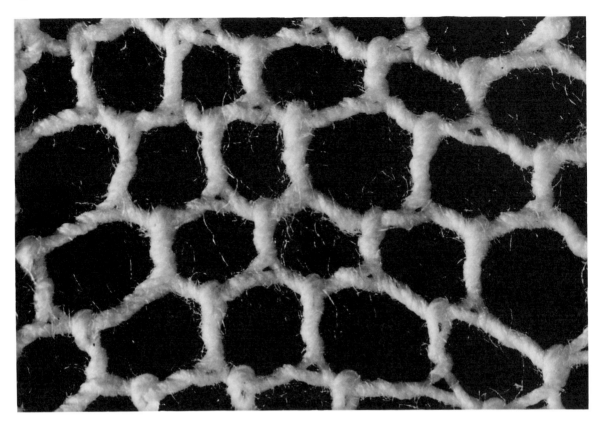

PHOTOGRAPH 92 *Wire-ground. (Also see* PHOTOGRAPH 6 *of early Branscombe Point)*

Wire-Ground

This is used for filling background spaces and can be found in early Branscombe Point lace. (*See* PHOTOGRAPH 6, page 14).

Regularity is important in the stitch.

The number of times the thread is coiled or overcast into the loops in the 2nd row depends on the distance between the stitches of the first row, and the thickness of the thread being used.

1st row: (*right to left*). Keeping the thread under your left-hand thumb, evenly space by making single buttonhole stitches with an extra twist and a slack loop between each stitch. Anchor the thread into the pinloop edge of the braid.

(*Left to right.*) Coil or overcast the thread over each loop between the stitches of the 1st row; 2, 3 or 4 times.

Space by overcasting along the edge of the braid.

Repeat.

Note: Working the 1st row from right to left and controlling the thread under your left-hand thumb, should make it easier to obtain regularity between stitches.

This stitch is also referred to as Greek Net stitch and Point de Tulle.

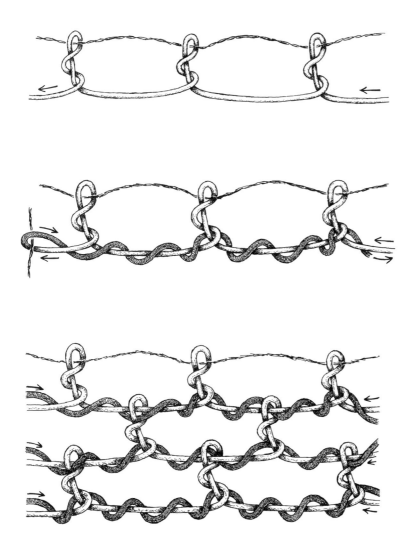

DRAWINGS 52A, B and C *Wire-ground*

Part 4

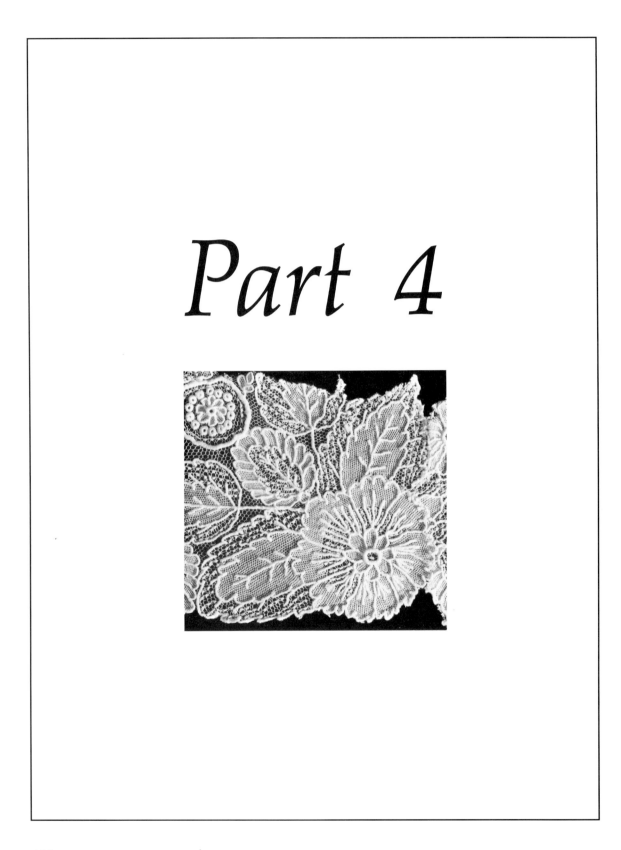

Patterns

All patterns are shown actual working size, unless otherwise indicated.

Beginners

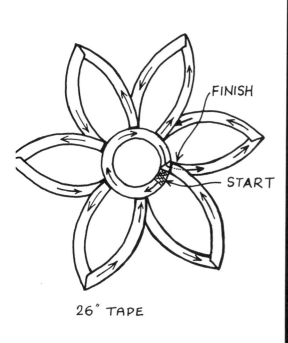

26″ TAPE

PATTERN 1 *(Reduced by 25%)*

FINISH — START

18" TAPE.

PATTERN 2 *Shown above, before being pressed with a hot iron on a damp cloth, and below, after being pressed with a hot iron on a damp cloth (diagram reduced by 25%)*

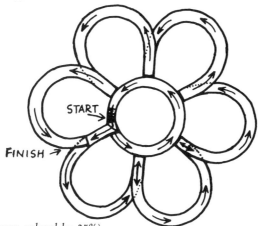

PATTERN 3 *(Diagram reduced by 25%)*

Traditional

PATTERN 4 *Handkerchief corner*
(diagram reduced by 25%)

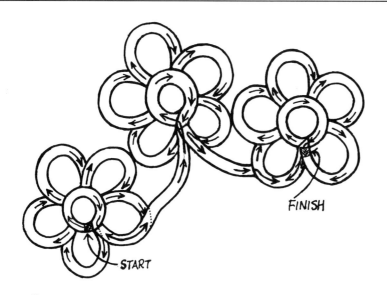

PATTERN 5 *Handkerchief corner*
(reduced by 25%)

PATTERN 6 *Handkerchief corner*
(reduced by 25%)

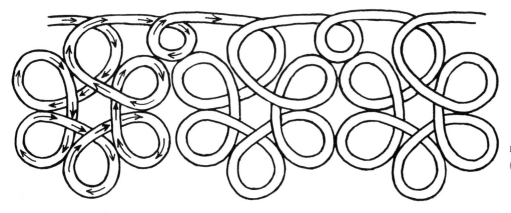

PATTERN 7 *Edging*
(reduced by 25%)

123

PATTERN 8 *Handkerchief*
(**see** PHOTOGRAPHS 26 *and* 27)
(*reduced by 25%*)

PATTERN 9 *The traditional Rose
and Tulip design (reduced by 25%)*

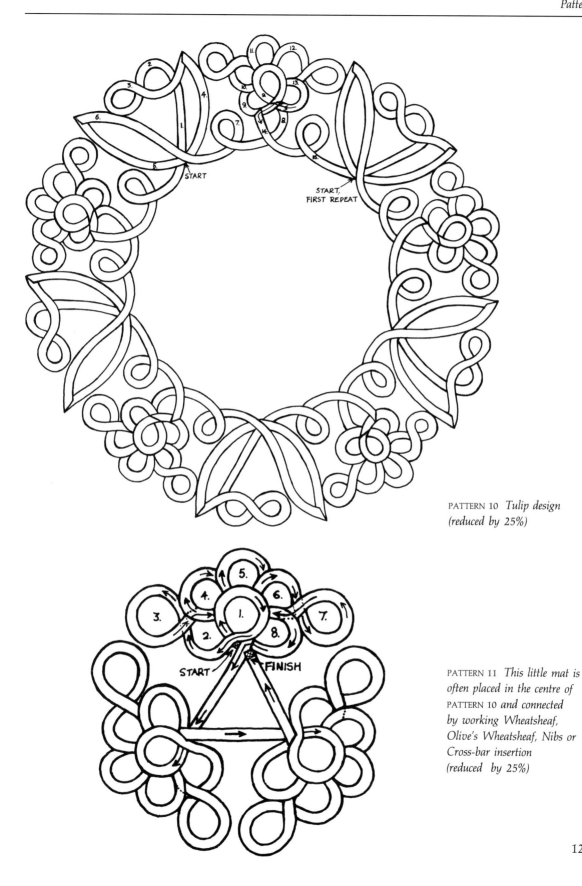

PATTERN 10 *Tulip design*
(reduced by 25%)

PATTERN 11 *This little mat is*
often placed in the centre of
PATTERN 10 *and connected*
by working Wheatsheaf,
Olive's Wheatsheaf, Nibs or
Cross-bar insertion
(reduced by 25%)

PATTERN 12 *A popular traditional design*

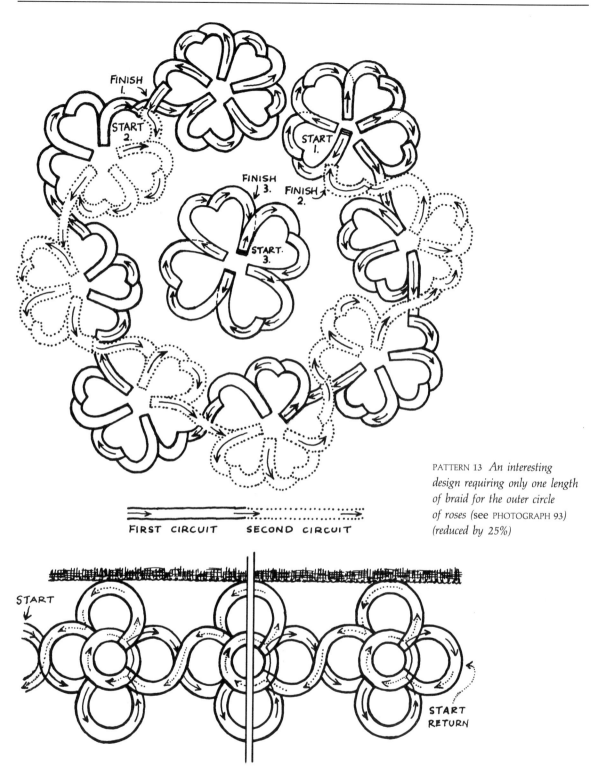

FINISH 1.
START 2.
START 1.
FINISH 3.
FINISH 2.
START 3.

FIRST CIRCUIT   SECOND CIRCUIT

PATTERN 13 *An interesting design requiring only one length of braid for the outer circle of roses (see* PHOTOGRAPH 93*) (reduced by 25%)*

START
START RETURN

PATTERN 14 *Edging, requiring one length of braid, tacked in the same way as* PATTERN 13 *(reduced by 25%)*

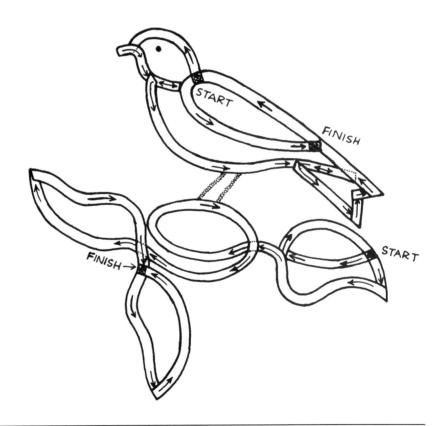

PATTERN 15 *Butterfly*
(reduced by 25%)

X X X X X = **2 LAYERS OF BRAID OVERLAPPING**

Modern

PATTERN 16 *Bird on nest*
(reduced by 25%)

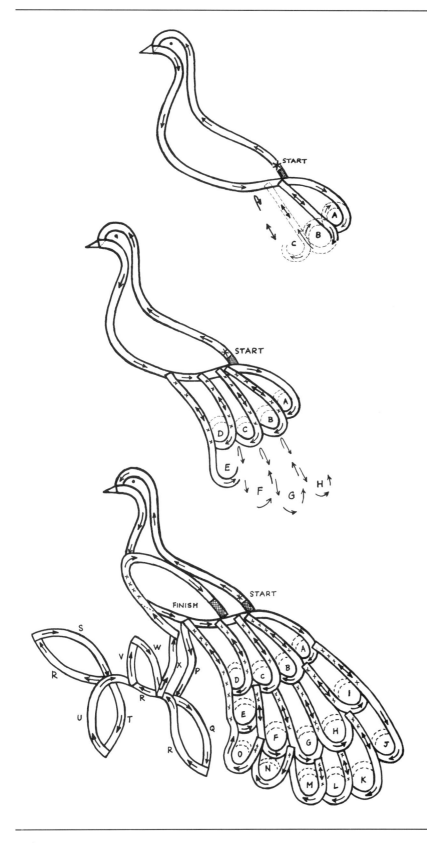

PATTERN 17 *Peacock*
(see DRAWINGS 1, 2 and 3
for working method)
(reduced by 50%)

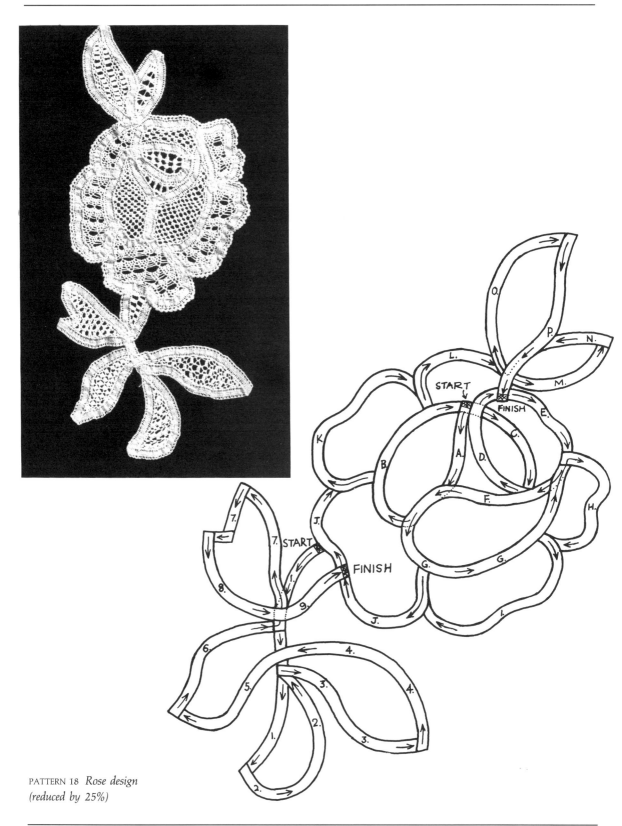

PATTERN 18 *Rose design*
(reduced by 25%)

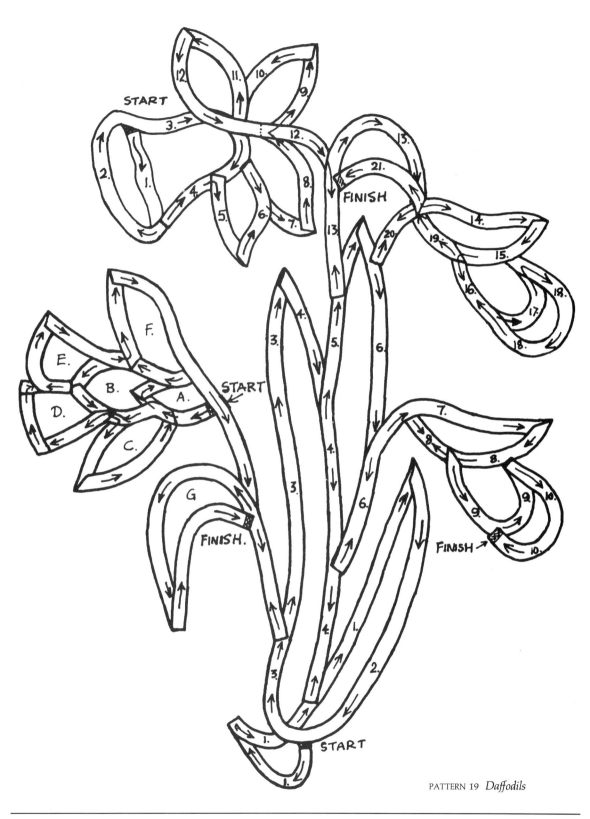

PATTERN 19 *Daffodils*

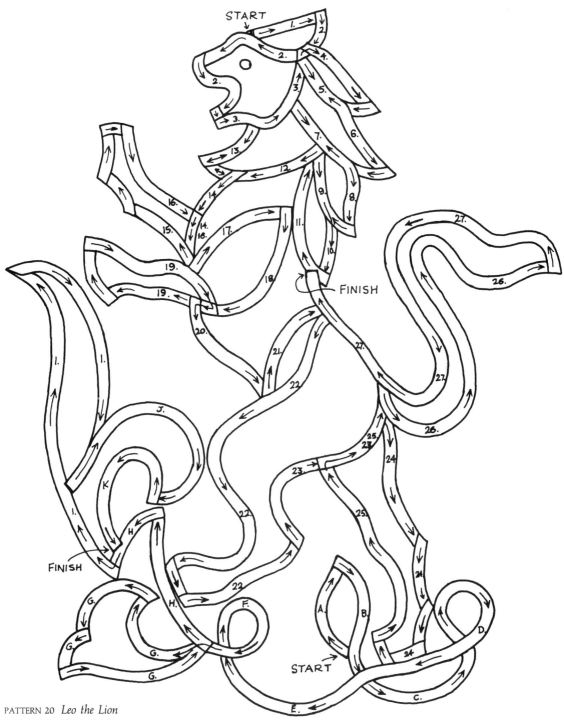

PATTERN 20 *Leo the Lion*
(reduced by 25%)

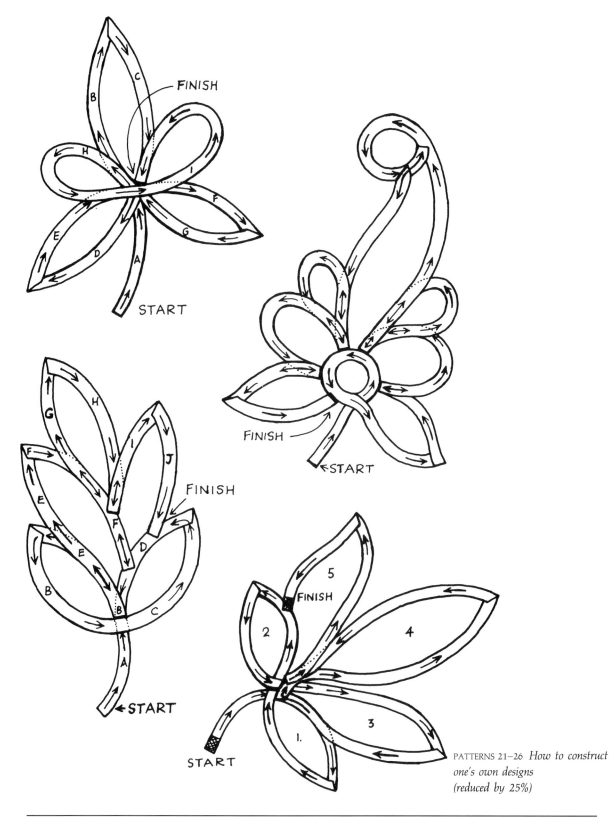

FINISH

START

FINISH

←START

START

FINISH

START

FINISH

PATTERNS 21–26 *How to construct one's own designs (reduced by 25%)*

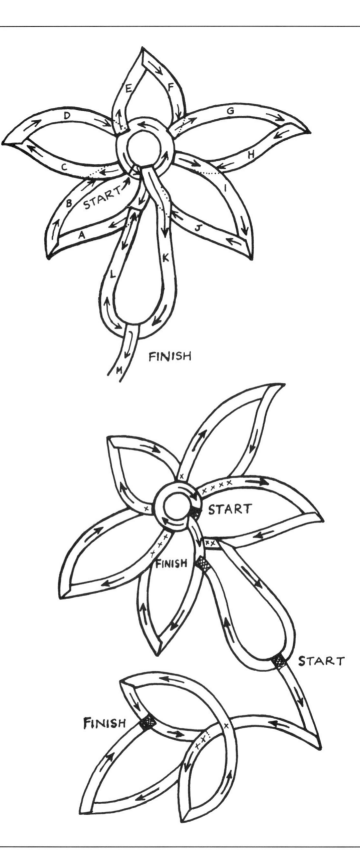

Collars

PATTERN 27
(reduced by 50%)

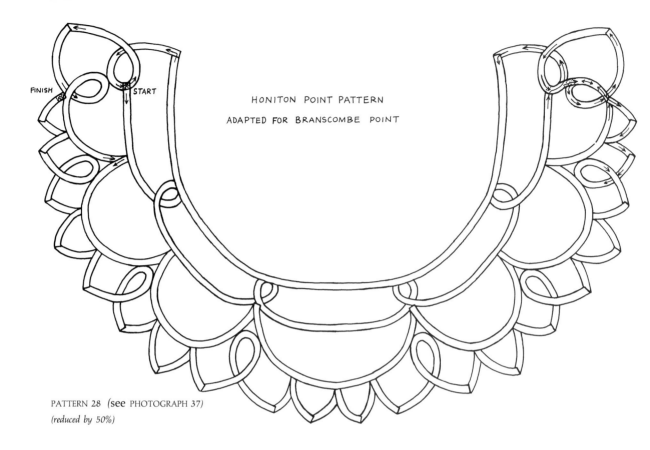

HONITON POINT PATTERN

ADAPTED FOR BRANSCOMBE POINT

FINISH

START

PATTERN 28 *(see* PHOTOGRAPH 37*)*
(reduced by 50%)

Mat

PATTERN 29 *A traditional pattern from Laura Somers and Miss Parrett (reduced by 30%)*

Examples of various needlepoint laces

PHOTOGRAPHS 93–107 show just a few examples of different types of needlelaces, to compare with Branscombe Point. To anyone interested

PHOTOGRAPH 93 *Traditional Branscombe Point, an interesting pattern, with just one length of braid used for the outer circle of roses.* (See PATTERN 13)

PHOTOGRAPH 94 *Early twentieth-century edging for window blinds, obtainable from furnishing shops. It was made by the shop assistants when business was slack, using coarse, heavy, machine-made braids, joined together with handmade buttonhole-stitch bars*

in lace, closer inspection of the actual design, working of the lace, and the stitches used are all part of the fascinating study of whether an example is needle made, bobbin made, machine made or another type of lace altogether. Studying the individual characteristics of various laces requires a good magnifying glass and infinite patience, but with the increasing interest now being shown in both making and collecting lace, it is becoming more difficult for those who collect, but do not make lace, to identify some specimens where lacemakers have mixed their techniques.

Most tape laces are stronger and harder wearing than the exquisite dainty laces such as bobbin lace but, for the designer, simple fillings are often far more effective than more elaborate fillings, especially if they are chosen to enhance the design or pattern.

PHOTOGRAPH 94 is a good example of early twentieth-century

PHOTOGRAPH 95 *English Hollie Point made in 1767, an insertion with a dense ground of buttonhole stitches worked with extremely fine thread. It was also made in Spain, Flanders and Italy and is often referred to as 'Church Work' or 'Church Embroidery'. It is the same stitch as Linen stitch with cord (or can be worked with an extra twist), but worked using very tiny stitches and an extremely fine thread*

edging, which was sold by the yard and became very popular for trimming the lower edge of window blinds. The lace used heavy machine-made braids, usually in a straw colour, and joined together with handmade buttonhole stitches. The braids were initially tacked onto a pattern by junior assistants, and the more experienced members of the staff would then connect the braids together by hand. The quality of those laced edgings varied considerably, according to the ability of the shop assistant concerned.

Since an early date, small bands of insertions have been put on christening gowns and bonnets. On the baby's bonnet insertion seen in PHOTOGRAPH 95 the date 1767 is worked within the insertion, although it is very difficult to see here. *A History of Hand Made Lace* by Mrs Neville Jackson and E. Jesurum (1900) refers to Hollie or

Holy Point worked for personal adornment by the Puritans, using Ecclesiastical emblems such as the Tree of Knowledge, Holy Dove and Annunciation Lily.

Youghal lace is said to owe its origins to the Irish potato famine of 1846. A Mother Superior, from Presentation Convent, taught children in her care to make this lace to help support their starving families.

Unlike Branscombe Point Lace, the outline of a Youghal lace pattern is made using a thick, cord-like thread, and it is this thick thread which gives the finished lace its well-known raised effect. The excellent designs, extremely even tension with shaded and raised effects, perfect workmanship, and regularity of the stitches make many pieces of this lace difficult to tell apart from some good pieces of machine-made lace.

PHOTOGRAPH 96 *Youghal – Irish needlepoint: a beautiful lace, giving shaded and raised effects, with excellent designs*

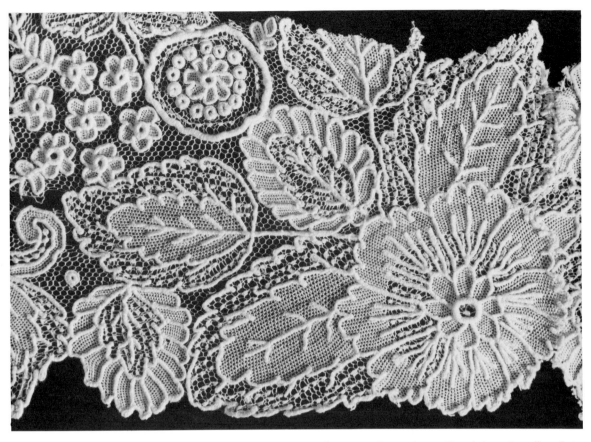

PHOTOGRAPHS 97 and 98 *Point de Gaze, a flimsy, dainty Flemish lace of excellent design, worked with very fine thread*

Point de Gaze differs from other needlepoint laces by the way in which the flower sprays are made on a pillow using a very fine thread, then assembled to form the design required and finally appliquéd onto exceptionally fine net. The raised effect in the design is formed by a thick thread (cordonnet) which is applied with evenly spaced single buttonhole stitches.

Many elaborate fillings are used in the completion of this lace. They are worked with a needle, as are the little spots which are always evident in Point de Gaze.

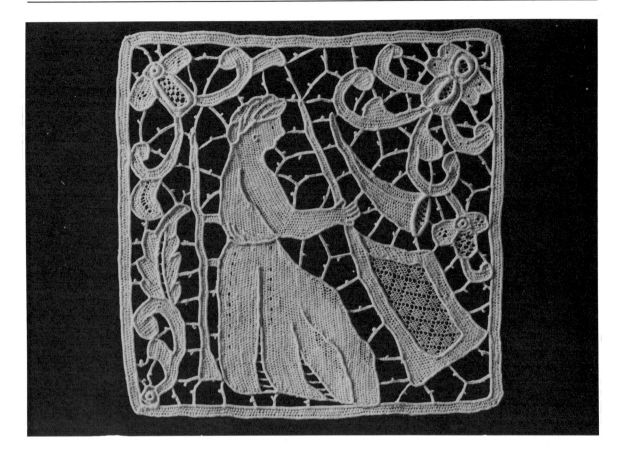

PHOTOGRAPHS 99 **and** 100 *Cyprus needlepoint of the late nineteenth or early twentieth century. Worked with a fairly coarse thread, this is a stiff type of lace, though not so stiff as Modern Cyprus, (*see PHOTOGRAPH 101*) which is made for the tourist trade*

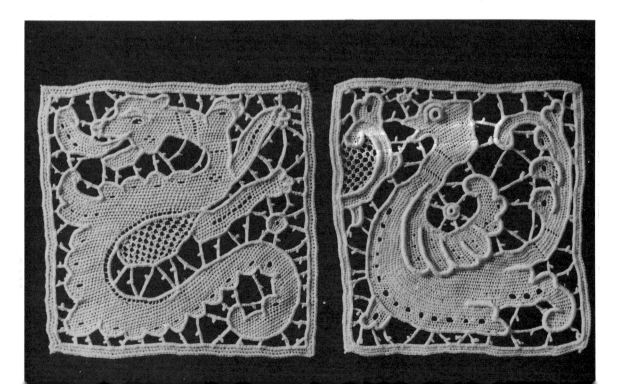

Cyprus needlepoint lace of the late nineteenth and early twentieth centuries was worked with a needle or tambour hook, using a fairly coarse thread and comprising closely knotted stitched worked over taut foundation threads.

The modern Cyprus lace seen in PHOTOGRAPH 101 shows the triangles worked with closely knotted stitches, but the diamond-shaped filling within the triangles is identical to Branscombe Point Double Knot filling using buttonhole stitch, as are the half-circles and bars, also with with closely worked buttonhole stitches.

PHOTOGRAPH 101 *Modern Cyprus needlepoint*

PHOTOGRAPH 102 *Maltese needlepoint of the early twentieth century. The fillings are worked with a fairly coarse thread and are of a softer texture than Cyprus needlepoint. The braid or tape similar to Branscombe Point*

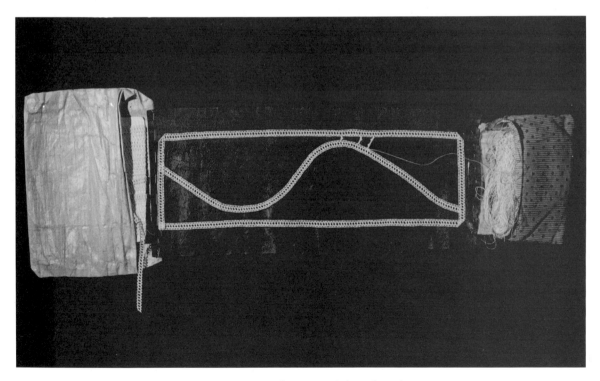

PHOTOGRAPH 103 *Italian Point of the eighteenth century*

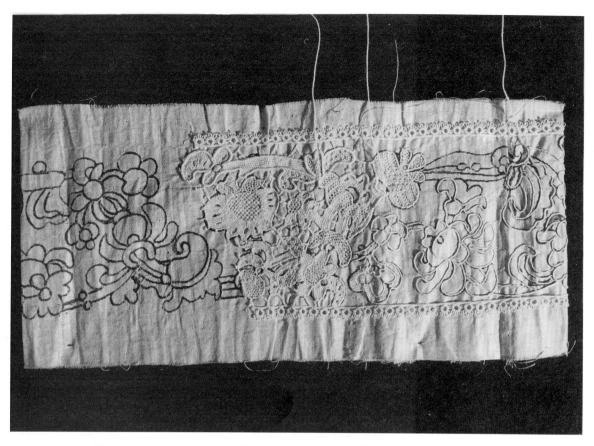

PHOTOGRAPH 104 *Note the attractive tatting edge being attached to the needlepoint*

PHOTOGRAPH 103 shows a design for Italian needlepoint lace of the eighteenth century, where the design has been drawn onto a piece of soft green leather using Indian ink. Note the pockets at either end of the pattern, one holding a fairly fine linen thread, and the other a good, straight-edged braid, which can be seen to have pin-holes similar to those on Branscombe Point braid.

Printed in Indian ink at the base of the design, but barely discernible in the photograph, are the words: *Italian Point 18th Century — thick with buttonhole edge.*

PHOTOGRAPH 104 also shows an Italian needlepoint design in the course of being made, with some interesting partially worked fillings. Note the attractive edge of tatting being attached to either side of this needlepoint insertion. Again, the design is drawn in Indian ink, but here glazed calico was used as the base material.

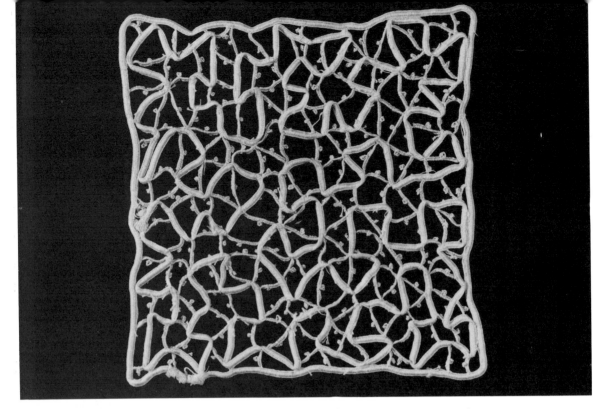

PHOTOGRAPHS 105A, B and C *Dickel lace, also known as Ardenza Point*

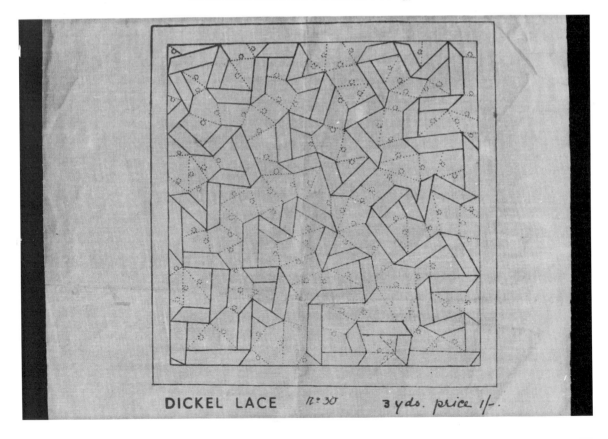

DICKEL LACE   N° 30   3 yds. price 1/-.

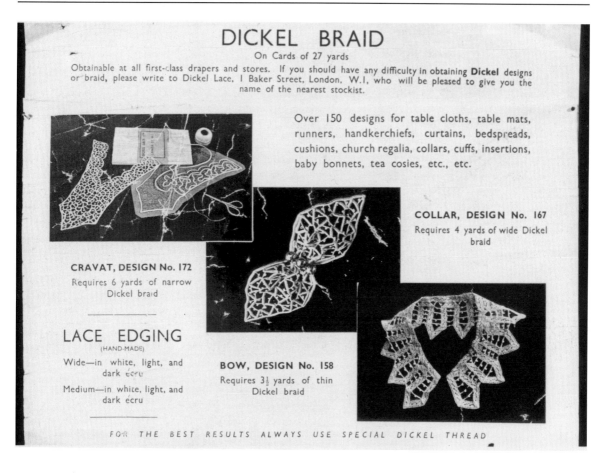

DICKEL BRAID
On Cards of 27 yards

Obtainable at all first-class drapers and stores. If you should have any difficulty in obtaining **Dickel** designs or braid, please write to Dickel Lace, 1 Baker Street, London, W.1, who will be pleased to give you the name of the nearest stockist.

Over 150 designs for table cloths, table mats, runners, handkerchiefs, curtains, bedspreads, cushions, church regalia, collars, cuffs, insertions, baby bonnets, tea cosies, etc., etc.

COLLAR, DESIGN No. 167
Requires 4 yards of wide Dickel braid

CRAVAT, DESIGN No. 172
Requires 6 yards of narrow Dickel braid

LACE EDGING
(HAND-MADE)

Wide—in white, light, and dark ecru

Medium—in white, light, and dark ecru

BOW, DESIGN No. 158
Requires 3½ yards of thin Dickel braid

FOR THE BEST RESULTS ALWAYS USE SPECIAL DICKEL THREAD

To make Dickel lace, patterns were clearly printed onto glazed calico, and then the braids tacked on. The braids are connected with closely worked buttonhole stitch bars with picots, to make a stiff type of lace.

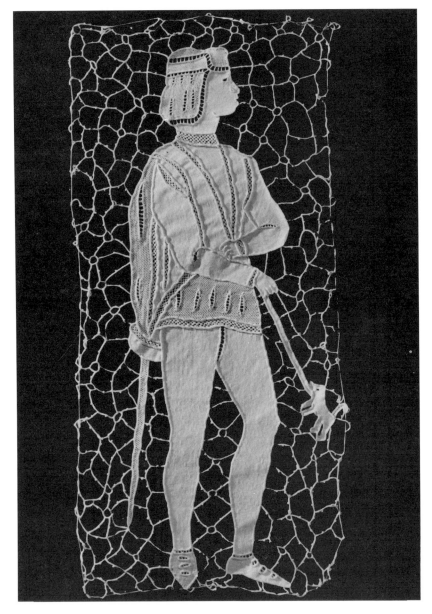

PHOTOGRAPHS 106 and 107 *Modern needlepoint lace with a mixture of techniques, from various types of lace. Made with fairly coarse, tightly spun thread of a silky appearance. The lace could be Chinese or Burano. It shows the characteristics of Venetian lace rather than Belgian*

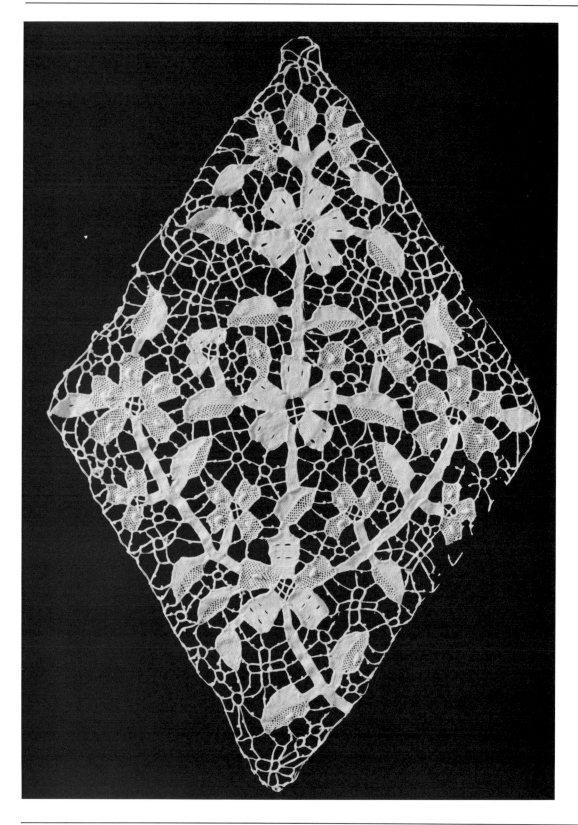

Bibliography

	Practical Point Lace, Weldon's 2d Magazines.
1874	*Antique Point and Honiton Lace*, Mrs Treadwin.
1880	*Dictionary of Needlework*, S.F.A. Caulfield & B.C. Saward.
1897	*Encyclopaedia of Needlework*, Thérèse De Dillmont, reprinted 1975.
1899	*Point and Pillow Lace*, Sharp.
1900	*The History of Handmade Lace*, E. Neville Jackson.
1901	*Modern Lacemaking – Advanced Studies*, The Butterick Publishing Co. Ltd.
1907	*Point Lace*, Wilkinson.
1908	*Chats on Old Lace*, E. Leigh Lowes.
1908	*Seven Centuries of Old Lace*, Mrs John Hungerford Pollen
1909–10	*Lace Making and Collecting*, an elementary handbook, A. Penderel Moody.
1923	*Lace in the Making*, Margaret L. Brooke, reprinted 1975.
1947	*A Manual of Lace*, Jeanette E. Petherbridge.
1958	*Anchor Manual of Needlework*, J. & P. Coats Ltd. (B.T. Batsford).

Suppliers and sources of information

Please note this is a general list for all types of lacemaking equipment etc.
Specialist Branscombe Point suppliers are listed on p. 155.

Specialist Branscombe Point suppliers are listed on p. 155.

UNITED KINGDOM

General suppliers

Alby Lace Museum
Cromer Road
Alby
Norwich
Norfolk NR11 7QE

Busy Bobbins
Unit 7
Scarrots Lane
Newport
IOW PO30 1JD

Chosen Crafts Centre
46 Winchcombe Street
Cheltenham
Glos GL52 2ND

Jo Firth
Lace Marketing & Needlecraft
  Supplies
58 Kent Crescent
Lowtown
Pudsey
W Yorks LS28 9EB

J. & J. Ford
October Hill
Upper Way
Upper Longdon
Rugeley
Staffs WS16 1QB

Framecraft
83 Hampstead Road
Handsworth Wood
Birmingham B2 1JA

R. Gravestock
Highwood
Crews Hill
Alfrick
Worcs WR6 5HF

The Handicraft Shop
47 Northgate
Canterbury
Kent CT1 1BE

Frank Herring & Sons
27 High West Street
Dorchester
Dorset DT1 1UP

Honiton Lace Shop
44 High Street
Honiton
Devon

D. J. Hornsby
149 High Street
Burton Latimer
Kettering
Northants NN15 5RL
  also at:
25 Manwood Avenue
Canterbury
Kent CT2 7AH

Frances Iles
73 High Street
Rochester
Kent ME1 1LX

Jane's Pincushions
Unit 4
Taverham Crafts
Taverham Nursery Centre
First Covert Road
Taverham
Norwich NR8 6HT

Loricraft
4 Big Lane
Lambourn
Berkshire

Needlestyle
5 The Woolmead
Farnham
Surrey GU9 7TX

Needlestyle
24–26 West Street
Alresford
Hants

Needlework
Ann Bartleet
Bucklers Farm
Coggeshall
Essex CO6 1SB

Needle and Thread
80 High Street
Horsell
Woking
Surrey GU21 4SZ

The Needlewoman
21 Needles Alley
off New Street
Birmingham B2 5AE

T. Parker
124 Corhampton Road
Boscombe East
Bournemouth
Dorset NH6 5NZ

Jane Playford
North Lodge
Church Close
West Runton
Norfolk NR27 9QY

Redburn Crafts
Squires Garden Centre
Halliford Road
Upper Halliford
Shepperton
Middx TW17 8RU

Christine Riley
53 Barclay Street
Stonehaven
Kincardineshire
Scotland

Peter & Beverley Scarlett
Strupak
Hill Head
Cold Wells
Ellon
Grampian
Scotland

Ken & Pat Schultz
134 Wisbech Road
Thornley
Peterborough

J. S. Sears
Lacecraft Supplies
8 Hillview
Sherington
Bucks MK16 9NY

Sebalace
Waterloo Mills
Howden Road
Silsden
W Yorks BD2 0NA

A. Sells
49 Pedley Lane
Clifton
Shefford
Beds

Shireburn Lace
Finkle Court
Finkle Hill

Sherburn in Elmet
N Yorks LS25 6EB

SMP
4 Garners Close
Chalfont St Peter
Bucks SL9 0HB

Southern Handicrafts
20 Kensington Gardens
Brighton
Sussex BN1 4AC

Spangles
Carole Morris
Cashburn Lace
Burwell
Cambs CB5 0ED

Stitchery
Finkle Street
Richmond
N. Yorks

Stitches
Dovehouse Shopping Parade
Warwick Road
Olton
Solihull
W Midlands

Teazle Embroideries
35 Boothferry Road
Hull
N Humberside

Lynn Turner
Church Meadow Crafts
15 Carisbrooke Drive
Winsford
Cheshire CW7 1LN

Valley House Craft Studios
Ruston
Scarborough
N Yorks

George Walker
The Corner Shop
Rickinghall
Diss
Norfolk

West End Lace Supplies
Ravensworth Court Road
Mortimer West End
Reading
Berks RG7 3UD

George White Lacemakers'
  Supplies
40 Heath Drive
Boston Spa
W Yorks L23 6PB

Christopher Williams
19 Morrison Avenue
Parkstone
Poole
Dorset

Bobbins

A. R. Arches
The Poplars
Shetland
near Stowmarket
Suffolk IP14 3DE

Bartlett, Caesar and Partners
12 Creslow Court
Stony Stratford
Milton Keynes MK11 1NN
  also at:
The Glen
Shorefield Road
Downton
Lymington
Hants SO41 0LH

T. Brown
Temple Lane Cottage
Littledean
Cinderford
Glos

Chrisken Bobbins
26 Cedar Drive
Kingsclere
Bucks RG15 8TD

Malcolm J. Fielding
2 Northern Terrace
Moss Lane
Silverdale
Lancs LA5 0ST

Richard Gravestock
Highwood
Crews Hill
Alfrick
Worcs WR6 5HF

Larkfield Crafts
Hilary Ricketts
4 Island Cottages
Mapledurwell
Basingstoke
Hants RG25 2LU

Loricraft
4 Big Lane
Lambourn
Berkshire

T. Parker
124 Corhampton Road
Boscombe East
Bournemouth
Dorset BH6 5NZ

Bryan Phillips
Pantglas
Cellan
Lampeter
Dyfed SA48 8JD

D. H. Shaw
47 Lamor Crescent
Thrushcroft
Rotherham
S Yorks S66 9QD

Sizelands
1 Highfield Road
Winslow
Bucks MK10 3QU

Christine & David Springett
21 Hillmorton Road
Rugby
War CV22 5DF

Richard Viney
Unit 7
Port Royal Street
Southsea
Hants PO5 3UD

West End Lace Suppliers
Ravensworth Court Road
Mortimer West End
Reading
Berks RG7 3UD

Lace pillows

Newnham Lace Equipment
15 Marlowe Close
Basingstoke
Hants RG24 9DD

Bartlett, Caesar and Partners
12 Creslow Court
Stony Stratford
Milton Keynes MK11 1NN
also at:
The Glen
Shorefield Road
Downton
Lymington
Hants SO41 0LH

Braids for Branscombe Point

The Honiton Lace Shop
44 High Street
Honiton
Devon

Tim Parker
124 Corhampton Road
Boscombe East
Bournemouth
Dorset BH6 5NZ

Silk embroidery and lace thread

E. & J. Piper
Silverlea
Flax Lane
Glemsford
Suffolk CO10 7RS

Silk weaving yarn

Hilary Chetwynd
Kipping Cottage
Cheriton
Alresford
Hants SO24 0PW

Frames and mounts

Doreen Campbell
Highcliff
Bremilham Road
Malmesbury
Wilts SN16 0DQ

Matt coloured transparent adhesive film

Heffers Graphic Shop
26 King Street
Cambridge CB1 1LN

Linen by the metre (yard) and made up articles of church linen

Mary Collins
Church Furnishings
St Andrews Hall
Humber Doucy Lane
Ipswich
Suffolk IP4 3BP

Hayes & Finch
Head Office & Factory
Hanson Road
Aintree
Liverpool L9 9BP

UNITED STATES OF AMERICA

Arbor House
22 Arbor Lane
Roslyn Hights
NY 11577

Baltazor Inc.
3262 Severn Avenue
Metairie
LA 7002

Beggars' Lace
P.O. Box 17263
Denver
Colo 80217

Berga Ullman Inc.
P.O. Box 918
North Adams
MA 01247

Frederick J. Fawcett
129 South Street
Boston
MA 02130

Frivolité
15526 Densmore N.
Seattle
WA 98113

Happy Hands
3007 S. W. Marshall
Pendleton
Oreg 97180

International Old Lacers
P.O. Box 1029
Westminster
Colo 80030

Lace Place de Belgique
800 S. W. 17th Street
Boca Raton
FL 33432

Lacis
2150 Stuart Street
Berkeley
CA 9470

Robin's Bobbins
RTL Box 1736
Mineral Bluff
GA 30559

Robin and Russ
Handweavers
533 North Adams Street
McMinnvills
Oreg 97128

Some Place
2990 Adline Street
Berkeley
CA 94703

Osma G. Todd Studio
319 Mendoza Avenue
Coral Gables
FL 33134

The Unique And Art Lace Cleaners
5926 Delman Boulevard

St Louis
MO 63112

Van Scriver Bobbin Lace
130 Cascadilla Park
Ithaca
NY 14850

The World in Stitches
82 South Street
Milford
N.H. 03055

AUSTRALIA

Australian Lace Magazine
P.O. Box 1291
Toowong
QLD 4066

Dentelles Lace Supplies
c/o Betty Franks
39 Lang Terrace
Northgate 4013
Queensland

The Lacemaker
94 Fordham Avenue
Hartwell
Victoria 3124

Spindle and Loom
Arcade 83
Longueville Road
Lane Cove
NSW 2066

Tulis Crafts
201 Avoca Street
Randwick
NSW 2031

BELGIUM

't Handwekhuisje
Katelijnestraat 23
8000 Bruges

Kantcentrum
Balstraat 14
8000 Bruges

Manufacture Belge de Dentelle
6 Galerie de la Reine

Galeries Royales St Hubert
1000 Bruxelles

Orchidée
Mariastraat 18
8000 Bruges

Ann Thys
't Apostelientje
Balstraat 11
8000 Bruges

FRANCE

Centre d'Initiations à la Dentelle
  du Puy
2 Rue Duguesclin
43000 Le Puy en Velay

A L'Econome
Anne-Marie Deydier
Ecole de Dentelle aux Fuseaux
10 rue Paul Chenavard
69001 Lyon

Rougier and Plé
13–15 bd des Filles de Calvaire
75003 Paris

WEST GERMANY

Der Fenster Laden
Berliner Str. 8
D 6483 Bad Soden
Salmünster

P.P. Hempel
Ortolanweg 34
1000 Berlin 47

Heikona De Ruijter
Kleoppelgrosshandel
Langer Steinweg 38
D4933 Blomberg

HOLLAND

Blokker's Boektiek
Bronsteeweg 4/4a
2101 AC Heemstede

Theo Brejaart
Dordtselaan 146–148
P.O. Box 5199
3008 AD Rotterdam

Magazijn *De Vlijt*
Lijnmarkt 48
Utrecht

SWITZERLAND

Fadehax
Inh. Irene Solca
4105 Biel-Benken
Basel

NEW ZEALAND

Peter McLeavey
P.O. Box 69.007
Auckland 8

SOURCES OF INFORMATION

UNITED KINGDOM

The Lace Guild
The Hollies
53 Audnam
Stourbridge
West Midlands DY8 4AE

The Lacemakers' Circle
49 Wardwick
Derby DE1 1HY

The Lace Society
Linwood
Stratford Road
Oversley
Alcester
War BY9 6PG

The British College of Lace
21 Hillmorton Road
Rugby
War CV22 5DF

The English Lace School
Oak House
Church Stile
Woodbury
Nr Exeter
Devon

The Museum of Costume and Lace
Rougemont House
Castle Street
Exeter
Devon

International Old Lacers
President
Gunvor Jorgensen
366 Bradley Avenue
Northvale
NJ 076647
United States

United Kingdom Director of
    International Old Lacers
S. Hurst
4 Dollius Road
London N3 1RG

Ring of Tatters
Mrs C. Appleton
Nonesuch
5 Ryeland Road
Ellerby
Saltburn by Sea
Cleveland TS13 5LP

BOOKS

UNITED KINGDOM

The following are stockists of the complete Batsford/Dryad Press range:

Avon

Bridge Bookshop
7 Bridge Street
Bath BA2 4AS

Waterstone & Co.
4–5 Milsom Street
Bath BA1 1DA

Bedfordshire

Arthur Sells
Lane Cove
49 Pedley Lane
Clifton
Shefford SG17 5QT

Berkshire

Loricraft
4 Big Lane
Lambourn

West End Lace Supplies
Ravensworth Court Road
Mortimer West End
Reading RG7 3UD

Buckinghamshire

J. S. Sear Lacecraft Supplies
8 Hillview
Sheringham MK16 9NY

Cambridgeshire

Dillons the Bookstore
Sidney Street
Cambridge

Cheshire

Lyn Turner
Church Meadow Crafts
15 Carisbrook Drive
Winsford CW7 1LN

Cornwall

Creative Books
22A River Street
Truro TR1 2SJ

Devon

Creative Crafts & Needlework
18 High Street
Totnes TQ9 5NP

Honiton Lace Shop
44 High Street
Honiton EX14 8PJ

Dorset

F. Herring & Sons
High West Street
Dorchester DT1 1UP

Tim Parker (mail order)
124 Corhampton Road
Boscombe East
Bournemouth BH6 5NL

Durham

Lacemaid
6, 10 & 15 Stoneybeck
Bishop Middleham DL17 9BJ

Gloucestershire

Southgate Handicrafts
63 Southgate Street
Gloucester GL1 1TX

Waterstone & Co.
89–90 The Promenade
Cheltenham GL50 1NB

Hampshire

Creative Crafts
11 The Square
Winchester SO23 9ES

Doreen Gill
14 Barnfield Road
Petersfield GU31 4DR

Larkfield Crafts
4 Island Cottages
Mapledurwell
Basingstoke RG23 2LU

Needlestyle
24–26 West Street
Alresford

Ruskins
27 Bell Street
Romsey

Isle of Wight

Busy Bobbins
Unit 7
Scarrots Lane
Newport PO30 1JD

Kent

The Handicraft Shop
47 Northgate
Canterbury CT1 1BE

Frances Iles
Hatchards
The Great Hall
Mount Pleasant Road
Tunbridge Wells

London

W. & G. Foyle Ltd
113–119 Charing Cross Road
WC2H 0EB

Hatchards
187 Piccadilly W1

Middlesex

Redburn Crafts
Squires Garden Centre
Halliford Road
Upper Halliford
Shepperton TW17 8RU

Norfolk

Alby Lace Museum
Cromer Road
Alby
Norwich NR11 7QE

Jane's Pincushions
Taverham Craft Unit 4
Taverham Nursery Centre
Fir Covert Road
Taverham
Norwich NR8 6HT

Waterstone & Co.
30 London Street
Norwich NR2 1LD

Northamptonshire

Denis Hornsby
149 High Street
Burton Latimer
Kettering NN15 5RL

SCOTLAND

Embroidery Shop
51 Willain Street
Edinburgh
Lothian EH3 7LW

Waterstone & Co.
236 Union Street
Aberdeen AB1 1TN

Staffordshire

J. & J. Ford
October Hill
65 Upper Way
Upper Longdon
Rugeley WS16 1QB

Sussex

Waterstone & Co.
120 Terminus Road
Eastbourne

Warwickshire

Christine & David Springett
21 Hillmorton Road
Rugby CV22 6DF

Wiltshire

Everyman Bookshop
5 Bridge Street
Salisbury SP1 2ND

North Yorkshire

Craft Basics
9 Gillygate
York

Shireburn Lace
Finkel Court
Finkel Hill
Sherburn in Elmet
N. Yorks LS25 6EB

Valley House Craft Studios
Ruston
Scarborough YO13 9QE

WALES

Bryncraft Bobbins (mail order)
B. J. Phillips
Pantglas
Cellan, Lampeter
Dyfed SA48 8JD

West Midlands

Needlewoman
Needles Alley
off New Street
Birmingham

West Yorkshire

Sebalace
Waterloo Mill
Howden Road
Silsden BD20 0HA

George White Lacemaking Supplies
40 Heath Drive
Boston Spa LS23 6PB

Jo Firth
58 Kent Crescent
Lowtown
Pudsey
Leeds LS28·9EB

Index

(*Note*: PH. = photograph(s); DR. = drawing(s); and PAT. = pattern(s).)